Purchasing Negotiations

Purchasing Negotiations

C. Wayne Barlow
Glenn P. Eisen

CBI PUBLISHING COMPANY, INC.
Russia Wharf
286 Congress Street
Boston, MA 02210

Printed in the United States of America.

Printing (last digit): 9 8 7 6 5 4 3 2 1

Library of Congress Cataloging in Publication Data

Barlow, C. Wayne.
    Purchasing negotiations.

    1. Purchasing 2. Negotiation in business. 3. Sales.
I. Eisen, Glenn P. II. Title
HF5437.B362   1983   658.7′23   82-14614
ISBN 0-8436-0881-1

To my wife Ruth, who has for many years been companion, confidante, gentle critic, and above all friend.

C.W.B.

To my lovely wife Karen, who taught me the value of negotiations in marriage; to my children, Julie and Steve, who taught me that negotiations are never easy, particularly when you get emotionally involved; and to the men and women of the purchasing profession with whom I have had the privilege of meeting, who have provided material and incentives I needed to write this book.

G.P.E.

Contents

Preface

The 1970s taught us that we needed to be very flexible—that unlimited supplies and long-term pricing were no longer a given condition in the market. The rate of technological change in the last decade was staggering, and purchasing people who did not make a dedicated effort to keep up found that they quickly became outdated. The statement "we survived the shortages of 1974" is still often heard as a measure of good past performance.

1974 was nine years ago. The problems and their accompanying solutions may no longer be important, except as a lesson in survival. The 1980s are presenting a new set of problems which are offering opportunities for purchasing professionals to develop unique solutions that can be implemented in today's economy. We cannot continue to live only by past success.

Some of the conditions we must deal with are double-digit inflation and unemployment. Companies that in the past were leaders in technology and productivity because they had more years of experience than their competitors are now suspected by their customers of becoming senile. One of the most important lessons the purchasing profession is learning is that a quotation often represents nothing more than a vendor's "going in" position.

Forward-thinking purchasing managers are becoming routinely involved in strategic planning. Their planning often takes the form of deciding the pricing position they want to assume (i.e., do they always want to pay the lowest available price?) and the degree and extent of commitment they seek with their vendors. Buyers are moving away from the historical adversary relationship between buyers and sellers to develop vendor subcontract networks. Strategies related to leveraging vendors' capabilities are becoming widespread—companies are reducing the total number of vendors they actively buy from and shifting storage inventory ownership to the lowest cost location, whether it's the buyer's or the seller's plant. Implementation of these strategies will result in a new environment for buyers and sellers. Final implementation will occur only when both buyers and sellers are satisfied, and their mutual satisfaction can best be achieved by negotiation.

This book was designed to be used as a resource, to assist readers in implementing their negotiation programs. We used our past experiences—what we learned from our failures and our successes—as the basic input. We feel that all the techniques we are presenting can be effectively used in purchasing. The selection of particular strategies for a specific situation will depend on the reader's needs, his or her organization's personality, and the nature of the commodities that are being purchased.

We want to continue to learn. We realize that situations will arise that are not covered by our book. Many of you have provided input to us by sharing your experiences—successes and failures. We hope this will continue in the future. If you, our readers, have experiences we have not addressed, please let us hear from you.

C. Wayne Barlow
Glenn P. Eisen

Purchasing Negotiations

1

The Role of Negotiation in Purchasing

The concept of purchasing that has prevailed for many years, i.e., all that was necessary was to get bids and then make the buying decision, no longer applies in today's marketplace. In almost any industry buyers face an array of problems that their predecessors never could have imagined.

Purchasing people now must deal in a world market. True, they may not be engaging directly in offshore buying, but the impact of happenings around the world is apparent. Those who do buy offshore are well aware of the mounting difficulties in doing so. The shortage years of 1973–1975 brought home a host of unpleasant facts. Many of the items thought to be available in the United States turned out to be of foreign manufacture. Purchasing departments were no longer in complete control of the buy-sell situation. There were no surplus markets where the buyer could pick and choose at will. The old concept of the bid system began to erode rapidly. Sellers became more aggressive as the demand for their products increased, creating the upward spiral of prices. Purchasing became a front-line bastion in the battle against inflation. When purchasing departments discovered that a number of the accepted ways of doing things were now ineffective, many chose expansion of their use of negotiation as the most progressive way to handle the situation.

Negotiation is not new. It has been an accepted part of life throughout history. Essentially, negotiation is a technique for communication of ideas wherein both parties are intent on convincing the other party to accede to their demands. The ultimate objective is to arrive at an agreement that will work to the benefit

1

of both parties. Negotiation is not an exact science in which specific rules and procedures can be laid down to guide the proceedings. As a result, no two negotiations will ever proceed in the same manner. Skill levels of the negotiators play a vital role in determining how successful each one will be. Disparities in the intellectual ability, knowledge, skills, and preparation of the negotiators make the art of negotiation the exciting activity that it is today. Most buyers who use negotiation consider it the really stimulating part of the purchasing job. Negotiation is a test of skills and a battle of wits.

REASONS FOR NEGOTIATING

"Why negotiate? If all factors are equal and the order is placed with the low bidder, isn't that enough?" That is the assumption made by too many buyers today. They do not see the need for or benefits that can be derived from negotiating. Some buyers claim that negotiating is not ethical because it gives unfair advantage to one supplier. Actually these are just excuses for not solving a problem.

What if there is only one source? How does the buyer know that he or she is getting everything the vendor is willing to offer? A buyer is naive if he or she assumes that a vendor will provide any more than what is necessary to be sufficiently competitive to get the order.

Buyer self-interest in providing management with an objective measurement of buying performance is an important reason to become a professional negotiator. It is difficult to develop buyer performance criteria that measure the actual buying job. Most criteria address clerical tasks such as number of purchase orders or requisitions processed. Realistic negotiation objectives that support the organization's business objectives can be established to serve as the criteria for buyer measurement. The degree of achievement of these objectives can be the measurement of the buyer as a professional.

It is becoming increasingly difficult to engineer the large cost-saving programs so readily available in the past. The buyer must now concentrate on two aspects of performance—cost avoidance and cost reductions. Both are viable targets of negotiation.

Cost avoidance is a primary reason for serious negotiation. The rate of change of technology offers many alternative methods of producing, pricing, or performing. The resulting benefit will usually be reduced or stabilized costs and more efficient methods of doing business.

Cost reduction has historically been the justification that buyers have used for the purchasing function. Too often cost reduction has been achieved by haggling or threatening a vendor with loss of business. True cost reduction, with continuance of vendor service and quality, can be achieved by reaching a negotiated agreement where the vendor benefits along with the buyer. Buying cheaper does not always mean buying better.

Cost Avoidance

The prices of equipment, supplies, and services that are needed by companies are composed of many elements. A vendor has to pay for labor, materials, operating expenses, and equipment and still make a profit. All services provided by a vendor have to be paid for by a buyer. Services may be in the form of technical assistance, engineering development, or warehousing. Quite often a buyer may actually pay for services given to the vendor's other customers because the vendor offers these services to all customers. For instance, if a vendor sells FOB delivered (the vendor pays the freight charges) to all customers, a buyer 50 miles from the vendor's plant ends up paying part of the freight charges for a customer 2000 miles from the vendor's plant.

Industry customs concerning overruns and quality can provide additional profit to the vendor at the buyer's expense. A 10 percent overrun of production can double a vendor's profit. If industry custom is plus or minus 10 percent, the buyer has no recourse if the overrun was not discussed before the order was placed. The discussion of cost negotiation in Chapter 2 illustrates how a 10 percent overrun affects the vendor's profit.

Cost Reduction

The traditional bid system is still useful for many types of purchases, but it is now being combined with negotiation to improve cost reduction. Many professional buyers use the bid as a device to keep the door open for potential suppliers. It is never wise to overly restrict opportunities for new suppliers to "get a look at the business." Restricting the source base is dangerous for long-term growth and overall purchasing performance. By using the bid system coupled with negotiation with the survivors, the buyer preserves the "open door" policy, yet eliminates those suppliers who are

a. Not technically equipped to do the job.
b. Not geographically located for the best performance.

By using the bid system as a screening device, the buyer can accurately determine which suppliers merit the process of negotiation. Since usually these are the low bidders, the buyer has an excellent starting point for negotiation.

To increase cost reduction, the buyer must think of the "cost of acquisition" and ownership rather than just the purchase price. In business today, the purchasing department in the average company will spend at least 50 percent of the sales dollar. The buyer must consider all of the factors that are cost items to the buyer's company, including freight charges, quality control costs, warehousing costs, purchase costs (paperwork and expediting), and the cost of money.

For the first time in years, the buyer must take into account the impact of purchases on the cash flow of the company. As an example, suppose the purchasing department has the opportunity to buy a product at a discount long before the product is needed. Before the buyer can make a relevant decision, he or she has to consider not only the cost of warehousing but also the cost of money to finance the purchase. The total analysis should include consideration of negotiating for free storage, delayed payments, and extension of terms.

Assurance of Supply

Governmental regulation, changing markets, and energy are three major factors that will affect the availability of materials in the 1980s. When shortages occur, vendors will have to decide which customers to serve first. A professional negotiator forecasts future requirements and plans for shortages. Anyone who survived the shortages of the 1970s knows that one cannot get all one needs without extra work. Negotiated agreements will help assure a continuing supply despite shortages.

Negotiations with sole sources of supply are possible. Negotiations between labor and management are always sole source, and the sides are usually able to reach mutually acceptable agreements.

Establishment of Relationships

Long-term buyer-seller relationships are desirable for both the buyer and the seller. The cost of bringing a new supplier to a company can range from a few hundred dollars to over $20,000. The cost depends on what the supplier is selling and the amount of work the buyer's company has to do to adjust to the new supplier. Some of the problems with new suppliers include quality, scheduling, and communications difficulties. The buyer can anticipate and resolve these problems through negotiation.

Vendors provide materials or services that the buyer's company would rather purchase than make or perform itself. If a supplier is manufacturing a product that is an integral component of the buyer's product line, the buyer must make sure the supplier is willing to accommodate the special needs of the buyer's company. Supplier sympathy for a buyer's "mistake" is often very limited, particularly if the supplier is not from North America.

Development of Standards of Performance

What is good performance? On-time delivery? No rejects? A low price? Each of these issues is open to negotiation. The special needs of a buyer's company must be discussed and agreed on before a vendor is authorized to start to work.

The best way to evaluate a vendor is for the buyer to agree with the vendor, in advance, on what is good performance and then to measure the performance against the agreement. Some agreements refer to a service level ("98 percent of all deliveries will be within forty-eight hours of the vendor's acknowledgment date") or to quality ("major functional rejects will not exceed 0.65 percent of the quantity delivered"). Qualified standards of performance allow for continuing measurement of vendor performance.

Avoidance of Problems

Few buyers do not have some sort of problem every Friday afternoon at about 3:00 P.M. The problem usually causes the buyer, the requisitioner, and the vendor to get upset. Since most problems are repetitive, it is possible to negotiate how problems will be solved and reduce them to just another part of the normal business relationship.

Problems are particularly likely to occur when buyers are unfamiliar with the customs of the vendor. The communications problems of international buying range from the language of the contract to proper interpretation of specifications. The United States' unwillingness to use the metric system has contributed to business communications problems throughout the world. Negotiation can ensure that all parties understand their responsibilities.

Survival in Today's Marketplace

The rate of change in technology is often too fast for companies to keep up to date. Companies must thus depend on their suppliers to keep them informed. Many companies have found themselves using old technology because their purchase agreements would not allow them to change to an updated part. This flexibility is essential in today's world.

Overcoming of Traditional Pricing

Many vendors have established "traditional" pricing practices that tend to be very restrictive. The opportunities to overcome price list pricing are improved when buyers negotiate. Many vendors are willing to talk about pricing policies and will often give concessions in the forms of alternative pricing or additional services if the buyer can convince the vendor that these concessions are to the vendor's advantage. The Robinson-Patman Act (see Chapter 6) does not forbid a vendor from making concessions to a customer who buys in a different manner from other customers.

FACTORS IN EFFECTIVE NEGOTIATION

The first factor in effective negotiation is accepting the importance of the negotiation process. Negotiating is not demeaning. Some buyers consider negotiating the same as haggling and view it as a poor business practice. They expect vendors to provide the best price and terms with the original quotation. However, vendors usually have some flexibility in what they are willing to provide in order to obtain business.

The difference between the profit on the original quotation and the profit required by the vendor's company is often significant. How many persons pay the list price of an automobile or the asking price of a home? Vendors will make concessions on such items as price, quality, service, etc., to buyers who are willing to negotiate. If the concessions are too large, a vendor can make up for the reduced profit through profit made from a buyer who considers negotiations demeaning.

Getting Started

Anger is one of the best ways to get a person started in negotiation. However, it is also the weakest position from which to negotiate because it tends to overshadow reason and logic. One cannot plan adequately when angry.

People do not like to look foolish. When a buyer finds that he or she could have gotten a better deal simply by asking for it, he or she is likely to feel angry. However, changing vendors out of anger is not a good policy.

Often the anger that teaches one to negotiate starts in personal life instead of in business. If you find out that a neighbor purchased the same automobile you did from the same dealer for $900 less, you get angry. Ideally, you also learned a lesson—the next time around, you question the price and negotiate.

When people become comfortable with negotiation in their personal life, they are able to use that same skill in business. The advantage of negotiating in business life rather than personal life is that the negotiator is asking the "embarrassing" questions for someone else. It is much easier to be a spokesperson for others.

Most people fear being rejected and look upon a "no" response as rejection. In negotiation, the "no" answer is not a rejection; it is merely an expedient way of saying that what was asked for is not possible at *this* time. Often the "no" changes to "possibly," to "maybe," to "I think so," to "yes." A good negotiator finds ways to get vendors to say "yes."

Most people are not natural negotiators. They are not prepared to respond to the opposition's arguments and are unable to turn these arguments to their advantage. Comfort in negotiations takes training, preparation, and discipline.

Being Prepared

In order to negotiate effectively, a negotiator must prepare properly. Preparation is often more important than one's conduct during the actual negotiations. The negotiator must establish objectives, determine a strategy, and evaluate the supplier's position before starting to negotiate. (Chapter 4, Planning for Negotiation, discusses in detail the methods of proper preparation.) Poor planning and anger are major causes of poor results in negotiation.

Gaining Respect

Many buyers feel that their vendors will not respect them if they negotiate. Others feel that vendors will simply raise their original prices to buyers who ask for lower prices; the vendor can then lower the price, making the buyer feel heroic because he or she negotiated a lower price. Both of these attitudes are incorrect.

Vendors respect a competent buyer who does not accept every proposal presented as "the best." A buyer who questions a vendor's facts forces the vendor to substantiate all facets of a proposal. Vendors have limited time and resources to provide all of the services their customers require. The buyer who asks for the services and points out how the vendor will benefit by providing them will normally receive the services requested. The amount and nature of the services received from the vendor are what negotiation is all about.

Buyers who are constantly asking for lower prices, without providing vendors corresponding benefits for lowering prices, are haggling, not negotiating. These buyers usually end up paying higher prices than buyers who get competitive bids and do no negotiating. But if true negotiation is demeaning and cheapens the business relationship, why is it that all governments and major businesses negotiate relationships as a standard practice?

Knowing What to Negotiate

Too often buyers assume that certain items are not negotiable because in the past vendors would not discuss these items or were unwilling to concede them. Today there is very little in the buying-selling relationship that cannot be negotiated. All steps in the purchasing cycle, from identification of the basic need for a product or service to final use of the product, are negotiable.

WHAT PURCHASING BUYS

The purchases of most buying departments can be classified into four general groups:

1. Construction and contractual services.
2. Capital machinery and equipment.
3. Inventory and support materials.
4. Maintenance, repair, and operational supplies.

Construction and Contractual Services

Measurable performance of labor makes construction and contractual service purchases distinctly different from all the other types. Although many contractual agreements involve the quality of "things" purchased, the major parts of the contract normally concern performance of labor.

With the exception of small service contracts (typewriter repair, certain types of equipment maintenance, etc.), most contractual agreements require a customized contract instead of a purchase order. Every aspect of the contract, from who prepares the final contract agreement to the rate of pay for overtime work, can be negotiated. Insurance liability, completion date, and quality of workmanship are major items that should be negotiated in all of these agreements.

Vendor selection is normally a joint effort of engineering, purchasing, and top management. Purchasing often plays the smallest role in the selection activities of the vendor selection team. However, the purchasing department does not have to be expert in the areas of purchase in order to lead the negotiation of the final terms of the agreement.

Capital Machinery and Equipment

Definition of what is a capital expenditure varies from company to company and according to Internal Revenue Service regulations. All depreciable assets having a useful life of over one year will be considered capital expenditures in this book.

Normally the selection of the type and manufacturer of the machine or equipment being purchased is up to the user. If a company has 200 Brand A typewriters or 50 Brand C milling machines, the unilateral substitution of an alternative brand by purchasing in order to get a better deal is not a wise decision. The final delivered cost of this type of purchase is only a portion of the total cost of the asset over its useful life.

Many vendors make little profit on their machinery. The majority of their profit comes from the continuing sale of parts, supplies, and maintenance services. Buyers willing to "discuss" all of the long-range aspects of capital purchases, including availability of spare parts many years after the installation, can often achieve concessions on the initial purchase.

Daily performance, reliability, and cost of operation are often the true measures of an asset's worth. Too many companies purchase equipment according to specification instead of performance. Creative performance negotiations that include measurements of future expectations and warranties are very beneficial.

Inventory and Support Materials

Inventory will be considered to be all items purchased by a manufacturer, distributor, wholesaler, or retailer for resale to a customer. It can refer to raw materials, assemblies, subassemblies, or finished goods. Inventories are normally sold for more than they cost, and they are considered as depreciable short-term assets of a company.

Support materials are those items that are purchased by a service company (bank, insurance company, hospital, etc.) or a government in order to provide the services required by their customers. They range from forms such as deposit slips, policy applications, and tax returns to products such as blood plasma and pillows. The cost of these products can be either included in or added to the price of the organization's services, depending on the nature of the service. The products are considered to be inventory by the organizations who own them.

Since all inventories are purchased in order to complete an organization's business cycle with its customers, the total investment in them, including the cost of owning, must be considered. The cost of *not* having certain types of inventory, such as deposit slips in a bank or wheel nuts in an automobile assembly plant, is often considerably higher than the actual cost of the materials.

A survey of U.S. purchasing operations conducted in 1979 showed that manufacturing companies spent four to twelve dollars on materials for every labor dollar. The fact that purchased materials often make up the *majority* of the sales dollar is a significant justification for a highly trained and competent purchasing operation. When the ratio of materials to labor is 10:1, a 1 percent material cost reduction is equivalent to a 10 percent labor cost reduction.

The role of the purchasing department in vendor identification and selection and in negotiation for inventory items is critical. Purchasing should be the major force in obtaining a final agreement with a company's inventory vendors. Every aspect of the daily business relationship between a company and its vendor is negotiable.

Professional buyers find ways to solve their employer's inventory problems; they don't make excuses for failures. All organizations have strategies that determine how they will market to their customers (these may be formal or informal). Inventory negotiations to support the strategies are easier to finalize than changes in the strategies. Few buyers are in a high enough position in the company to convince top managers that their strategies are not feasible.

Maintenance, Repair, and Operational Supplies (MRO)

Every organization needs supplies to operate its business. These supplies range from paper for a copying machine to spare parts and lubricants for machinery and equipment. MRO can also include the advertising brochures and premiums used by the sales department. Normally payments for these supplies are all classified as expenses. The costs are generally absorbed into the company's operating expenses in the period in which they are accrued. The MRO category of purchases usually requires more paperwork and more time than any other category of purchase.

Many of purchasing's problems, such as backdoor buying and selling, complaints about poor purchasing response, receipt of materials without proper paperwork, and internal audit complaints about purchasing's failure to follow procedures, result from MRO types of purchases. The Friday afternoon emergency that most companies have is often an MRO emergency.

Properly negotiated systems contracts, blanket orders, and other types of supply agreements can reduce paperwork and costs of supply. These agreements can also enhance purchasing's political position in the organization because they usually result in improved service to the requisitioner. Negotiations relative to such contracts often focus on solving the daily problems of buying rather than on achieving price reduction. In some cases these contracts may delegate the ordering of materials, as differentiated from the buying, to authorized requisitioners.

WHO ARE THE VENDORS?

Vendors fall in many categories. They may be manufacturers, distributors, wholesalers, brokers, retailers, manufacturers' representatives, contractors, or service companies. The type of company, the nature of the industry, and the personalities of the vendors determine how negotiations are conducted. In the following sections, we define the major categories of vendors with whom U.S. buyers are doing business today. The type of knowledge required of the negotiator and the kind of strategy for negotiation are often determined by the category of the vendor involved.

The Commodity Source

The commodity source sells exactly the same product or service, without modification, to each customer. If a customer does not need a certain item, the commodity source can normally sell that

exact item to another customer. Some typical items sold by commodity sources are office supplies, maintenance supplies, and
standard machinery. Generally, distributors and wholesalers are
commodity sources. Most companies would not consider manufacturing the materials they buy from commodity sources because a
company's total usage of one material generally is nowhere near
large enough to merit production of the item. Self-production of
an item that is readily available from a vendor's inventory is rarely
economical.

A second source of supply can usually be found for most commodities. The price differential between two commodity vendors
for the same item often is not significant. Differences in quality,
particularly between two distributors or wholesalers of the same
manufacturer, are often nonexistent. In addition to cost reduction, the buyer's objectives in vendor selection and negotiation
should be to improve the levels of service and to reduce the cost of
inventory by making warehousing arrangements.

The Capability Source

A vendor who produces a custom product for the customer is
called a capability source. The product cannot be easily resold if it
is rejected. An error on the part of the vendor or purchaser is usually costly to the party making the error unless the error is corrected before production starts.

Companies use capability vendors rather than producing for
themselves when the vendors are better able to produce what the
buyer needs. This higher capability may relate to pricing, quality,
or one of the other elements of the business relationship. When a
company finds that the cost of purchasing certain items exceeds
the amount it is willing to pay, it often considers producing them
itself. Make-or-buy analyses normally involve materials purchased
from capability sources of supply.

International Vendors

When buyers have to buy from vendors outside of their country,
they must learn to conduct negotiations according to customs with
which they are unfamiliar. Business customs vary from country to
country and even within regions of certain large countries, including the United States.

American buyers often have a great deal of difficulty
negotiating with overseas vendors because of their unfamiliarity
with the vendors' "rules" of business. It is important to know these
practices, because the settlement of claims in international courts

is costly and time-consuming. The United States and Canada are the only countries of the world where negotiation is not a part of daily life. Outside of North America, vendors expect buyers to negotiate. Negotiation is not merely a way of securing a better deal for the company, but the only way to conduct a business arrangement.

Distributors and Wholesalers

The role of distributors in U.S. business is very important. Without distributors many small companies would not be able to get the materials they need to stay in business.

Distributors buy from manufacturers at the manufacturers' list price less a distribution discount. They then resell the products at the same price as the manufacturer would give to a buyer of the particular quantity being purchased. If a buyer purchases in the same quantities as the distributor, he or she can often get the same price as the manufacturer would give, plus have the benefit of local warehousing.

Distributors provide a sales force and regional warehousing for manufacturers who do not want to perform these functions themselves. Distributors also service the many small customers that cannot purchase from a vendor because their orders are too small. Many large companies have set up distributors within their own company to service their small customers. Many distributors are family-owned businesses which service a limited region of the country.

Buyers who refuse to use distributors are often overlooking major opportunities. Distributors, particularly those that are family-operated, are often more flexible than the original manufacturer in their ability and willingness to negotiate.

Brokers

Brokers are independent business persons who sell the products of various manufacturers. Normally brokers will purchase from a manufacturer, mark the price up with a profit margin, and sell to a final customer. The shipment normally goes from the manufacturer to the customer. A broker has the ability to provide customers with the resources of many manufacturers. Often a broker can find manufacturers that a buyer is unable to locate.

Since brokers depend totally on customer satisfaction and the continued good will of the manufacturers, they tend to be open to negotiation. The final price paid to a broker is not necessarily higher than the price that would be paid to the manufacturer, since many manufacturers consider brokers to be their sales force and reduce their prices for the brokers.

Manufacturer's Agents

Manufacturer's agents generally function as brokers, in that they are independent business persons. The products they sell are those of the manufacturers they represent. Their billing is usually through the manufacturer, and they are paid a standard commission for the products they sell.

A manufacturer will usually use manufacturer's agents instead of a salaried sales force to avoid the internal cost of employing a full-time sales force. The agents receive compensation only when an order is shipped.

The company represented by the agent is normally bound by the agent's commitments unless restrictions placed on the agent are public knowledge. Negotiating with the company's agent is the same as negotiating with the company. A buyer should always make sure that the agent has the authority to commit the company he or she is negotiating for.

Trading Companies

As trade increased between the United States and Japan, U.S. business persons became familiar with an organization known as a trading company. Trading companies perform the marketing, financing, and buying functions of many companies in the Far East. Trading companies represent many diversified industries and even competitors within the same industry. Competing trading companies may represent the same manufacturer.

Companies that use trading companies depend on them for all of their relationships with the business world outside of their company. In Japan, almost all business is conducted through trading companies. Many Japanese banks also function as trading companies. Trading companies have a great deal of influence over the final selling prices established by the companies they represent.

The representatives of trading companies are qualified negotiators with extensive experience in negotiating all sorts of contracts. A buyer who does not prepare well before negotiating with a trading company will usually receive few concessions.

SUMMARY

Negotiations are serious business. The difference between an order placer who receives three bids and places an order with the low bidder and a professional buyer who pursues the best deal for the company through effective negotiations is significant. As the levels of technology and complexities of doing business increase, there will only be room for professional buyers in purchasing. Negotiations should be an essential part of the successful consummation of every business arrangement.

A buyer should have no difficulty justifying the need for negotiation. There are many potential benefits for the company and the buyer. These include improved ability to deal with changing world economic problems of inflation or recession, emerging and/or changing technology, materials availability, future problems and relationships, and traditional pricing and selling patterns. Possibly the most important justification a buyer should consider is his or her own self-interest in improving professional competency.

Negotiation can be conducted for all types of purchase categories, including:

- Construction and contractual services,
- Capital machinery and equipment,
- Inventory and support materials, and
- Maintenance, repair, and operating supplies.

There are very few instances where negotiation cannot improve the terms of the purchase.

The skills required of an effective negotiator can be easily learned if the buyer is willing to be receptive to new ideas. The buyer must sit down and plan in advance which items can be conceded to the vendor and which are essential. An understanding of the vendor's objectives will provide the buyer with the ability to negotiate an effective contract and help him or her persuade the vendor to say "yes."

There are two major categories of vendors with whom buyers do business—commodity and capability. Commodity vendors sell a standard product to all of their customers. Capability vendors sell a customized product to each customer. The vendor category and type of vendor company (manufacturer, distributor, broker, etc.) should influence the definition of negotiation issues and methods.

A positive mental attitude on the part of the negotiator is absolutely essential for success. A negative attitude, anticipating failure, will generally guarantee failure. A well-planned strategy, properly implemented, will usually result in success.

All negotiations should result in a mutually acceptable agreement. Such an agreement is the major objective of all negotiations.

2

Types of
Negotiations

All negotiations are not the same, even if they have the same general objective of reaching a mutually acceptable agreement. Economic conditions, the nature of purchases, vendor locations, and the resources available at any specific time affect what type of negotiation should be conducted. The amount of planning required and the types of strategies employed are determined by the type of negotiation.

Price negotiation is the most common type of purchasing negotiation. The factor under discussion is the vendor's selling price, including the impact of quantity, quality, and services performed. The majority of negotiations in industrial purchasing are price negotiations.

In *cost negotiation,* the various cost factors that enter into the final selling price are negotiated. These factors include labor, materials, overhead, administrative costs, profit, and the methods of production. The amount of knowledge and preparation necessary for this type of negotiation is considerably greater than that needed for price negotiation; the resultant benefits are usually correspondingly greater. This type of negotiation is common in Japan today, and will be used increasingly in the United States in the 1980s.

Because of changing business conditions the *renegotiation of an existing contract* often becomes necessary before the expiration date. As with labor contracts, reaching a new agreement is often a more desirable option than cancelling the contract or forcing the vendor to conform to the terms of the original. It is common in

17

many contracts to have a "reopener clause" that allows for re-negotiation.

In *one-on-one negotiation*, a buyer and a salesperson meet to negotiate a final agreement. Normally this type of negotiation cannot be finalized without additional approval because of limits of authority. Daily relations with suppliers, in which broad discussions of future business relationships are conducted, can be considered one-on-one. Too often vendors are well prepared for these meetings while buyers are not.

Team negotiation is the accepted practice for governmental and labor negotiations. The negotiating team is composed of people selected for their ability to contribute to, influence, or otherwise impact on the discussions. When the proper team is selected, the negotiations usually lead to a final agreement. Vendors may use team negotiation as a general practice.

The techniques, strategies, and customs for conducting *international negotiation* are very different from those for domestic business agreements. International purchasing requires a preplanning focus directed more to the personality aspects of the vendors. In order to effectively negotiate, a buyer needs to understand how the international vendor looks at doing business and to gain a feel for the vendor's cultural background and customs. The buyer must also overcome any personal prejudices that he or she may have. The terms and conditions of international contracts often differ from those of domestic contracts; these must be clearly understood and documented. Conducting research on a particular vendor's background may be very difficult—buyers often need outside assistance from consultants or governmental agencies to conduct this research.

Each type of negotiation will be discussed in greater detail in this chapter. Buyers who do not consider what type of negotiation is required will probably overlook many of the possibilities for gaining concessions from their vendors. Negotiation is not something that just happens.

Normal procedure in most purchasing departments is to obtain competitive quotations, whenever possible, before placing a purchase order. In most cases the buyer can make a commitment based on the low bid if "all factors are equal." Problems arise if all factors are not equal or if the buyer wants (or must obtain) a better "deal."

The reasons for requiring a deal better than one quoted are many. They include:

1.   Vendors are unwilling to quote the way a buyer wants to buy.

2. All quotes received are too high.

3. A creative vendor provides an alternative that is beneficial to the buyer's company.

4. Only one source is available.

5. The buyer is not sure what concessions vendors are willing to give and therefore wants to negotiate with several vendors to develop the best contract possible.

6. A degree of flexibility is allowable in the specifications and the buyer wants to use this for negotiating leverage.

There are, of course, many other valid reasons for entering into negotiation.

PRICE NEGOTIATION

The majority of negotiations in which a buyer will be involved can be considered price negotiations. Price negotiation is concerned with how what a buyer receives from a seller affects the selling price. This differs from cost negotiation in that the latter includes discussions of the vendor's costs of doing business and requires a cost analysis for every element of price.

During price negotiation buyers discuss the services and items they want to buy and sellers discuss the cost of providing these services and items. Negotiations revolve around what is a "fair" price for concessions. The topics to negotiate include total price, terms, allowances, tooling and plate costs, special services, quality requirements, packaging, transportation, delivery schedule or lead times, and other elements of the business cycle.

Price negotiation is relatively easy to plan for because the buyer can establish a set of objectives (see Chapter 4) based on past experience and readily available market information. The technical support required to assist the buyer is minimal because in-depth analyses of vendors' methods are not required. Pricing data are usually easily obtained from competitive bids and published indices. Trend analysis is an easy way to determine pricing history and make forecasts.

Price negotiation has certain disadvantages. Many vendors have used traditional pricing practices for many years, basing their prices on industry customs and what other customers have been willing to pay. These traditions are hard to defeat in price negotiation.

Another disadvantage of price negotiation is the "Robinson-Patman" excuse used by many vendors as a reason for not making concessions. They may claim that they would have to make the same concession to all of their customers. That claim is not always true, particularly when the buyer is able to buy in a different manner from all of the other customers.

COST NEGOTIATION

As we mentioned earlier, cost negotiation is concerned with the elements of vendors' costs that comprise a selling price. Buyers and sellers negotiate how prices are to be determined, how costs are to be calculated, and what alternatives might be considered in an effort to produce the desired product or service at the lowest overall cost.

The price paid to a vendor is composed of several elements. These include costs for materials, labor, overhead, general and administrative expenses, and profit. The methods used to determine these costs vary among vendors. The cost of materials and labor can vary widely, depending on how efficiently the vendor's purchasing and manufacturing departments operate. The percentage allocation of overhead, general and administrative costs, and profits can often be negotiated if the buyer is able to intelligently discuss these costs. The impact of traditional pricing practices on a vendor's profit is shown in the following case study on pricing.

CASE STUDY: Buyer A obtained a quotation for 1,000,000 printed brochures from Vendor B. The vendor's cost sheet for the proposal follows:

Paper (1 million plus scrap allowance @ 10%)	$10,000
Ink (to set up, print, and allow for problems)	1,000
Printing plates (customer artwork and film extra)	1,000
Machine set-up labor (4 hrs @ $15/hr × 2 persons)	120
Machine operating labor (12 hrs @ $10/hr × 4)	480
Finishing and packing labor (8 hrs @ $5/hr × 2)	80
Factory overhead @ 100% of labor	680
Total manufacturing costs	$13,360

General and administrative costs @ 100% of direct	13,360
Total cost of sale	$26,720
Profit @ 10%	2,672
Total selling price	$29,392

Quoted selling price $29.39 per thousand

Vendor B received the purchase order and ordered the paper, ink, and plates. The paper vendor delivered a 10 percent overrun. Vendor B printed the brochures and shipped 1.1 million pieces. Since "industry custom" allows for a 10 percent overrun, the vendor billed the entire quantity shipped at the $29.39 per thousand, or $32,329.

The vendor's total additional cost was the 10 percent extra for the paper, or $1000. The vendor's total profit was $4609: $2672 on the 1 million and $1937 on the 10 percent overrun.

The vendor's profit on sales for the original 1 million was 9.09 percent ($2672 divided by $29,392). The final profit on the job was 14.26 percent (4609 divided by $32,329).

In the case study Buyer A could have saved the company money by negotiating the cost of the overrun before making the purchase commitment.

Another factor that can be negotiated is labor rate changes. In the case study the labor cost was $680 total. If the cost of labor were to go up by 20 percent or $136, the selling price would increase by $449. The reason the increase is so large is that the following amounts are added by standard accounting practice:

overhead	$136
general and administrative	272
profit	41

Other negotiable costs include direct materials costs, direct labor costs, factory overhead, and general and administrative expenses.

The *direct materials cost* is the net cost of the raw materials used by a vendor. This includes all of the factors buyers use in determining cost, such as freight charges, discounts, inspection costs, etc. Buyers often find that they can supply raw materials to their vendors at a lower net cost than the vendor is charging.

Direct labor cost is the portion of the payroll cost that is paid to workers who are directly involved with converting the raw materials to a finished product. The method for determining exactly which workers are the "direct labor" can vary between companies. If a vendor intends to include the cost of engineering and production control in direct labor, the buyer should make sure that the vendor has accurate time reports which allocate the time to a job and that the vendor is not charging the buyer for the time again in general and administrative expenses.

A portion of a seller's overall manufacturing costs, *factory overhead*, is usually allocated to every product produced. These routine costs are in addition to the costs of labor and materials. Buyers can examine the allocation and details of overhead to ensure that they are not paying too much. Buyers should also be aware of the impact on overhead of percentage increases in direct costs, as shown in the previous labor rate increase example.

The elements of factory overhead include:

a. Indirect materials costs—expenditures for supplies, lubricants, and other materials needed to operate a factory.

b. Indirect labor costs—labor costs that are accrued as a result of down time, vacation allowances, supervision, materials handling, shipping, receiving, timekeeping, etc. Overtime is often an indirect labor charge. If a vendor produces during overtime hours, a buyer might want to examine the reasons for the extra time and ask for a waiver of the overtime charges.

c. Payments for power, light, heat, and rent.

d. Expenditures for maintenance and repair of machinery and buildings (factory facilities only) to keep them in good working order. New additions, improvements to existing facilities, and new equipment should be considered as capitalized costs and not as overhead (see depreciation of capital costs).

e. Insurance premiums for manufacturing facilities.

f. Taxes, except for those paid by manufacturing employees on their income. If a vendor is paying sales taxes for the purchase of energy used as part of a manufacturing process, such as heat treating or injecting molding, the buyer should suggest that the vendor apply for an exemption from these taxes. This will reduce overhead costs.

g. Depreciation and amortization of facilities, machinery, and equipment. Often a standard depreciation rate is applied to all production. This standard rate can have a major impact on the price paid by a buyer who is buying a labor-intensive product from a machine-intensive vendor.

h.   Other manufacturing expenses for training time, incentive bonuses, telephone calls, or perishable tools are also allowable overhead expenses.

General and administrative expenses are those operating expenses of a company that are not clearly identifiable. These generally include the operation of departments such as accounting and purchasing, management information services, and executive management.

In many companies accounting allocates general and administrative costs by calculating the total cost and assigning a portion of that cost to each unit of product sold. The allocation is usually based on a percentage of the volume of sales forecast for the year. If a company's volume increases disproportionately to administrative expenses, the company can make a profit on the allocation of the expenses.

Many vendors calculate a standard selling expense for each unit of product. If selling expense is not negotiated, large-volume buyers may be paying for vendor servicing of small-volume accounts.

When Cost Negotiation Makes Sense

Significantly more preparation and negotiation time is required for cost negotiation than for price negotiation. Normally it is not practical to use cost negotiation for all negotiations. However, in any of the following situations, cost negotiation should be considered.

Vendors who are designing custom products generally have many options in the design and production methods used. The use of standard components, rather than custom components, and the use of components whose useful life does not exceed the total life of the product are two major considerations that can have significant impact on cost. Products that can be produced on a variety of machines offer negotiation opportunities that often are not considered. Buyers can negotiate the methods of production with vendors.

Buyers can often calculate the vendor's raw material costs independently of the vendor. This is especially true for chemicals, steel, and paper products. Processing costs for many industries are published so the buyer can calculate these costs too.

A major problem facing many buyers is the lack of alternative sources of supply for certain products. In order to develop second sources of supply, buyers can often "assist" a vendor in developing the qualifications to produce a part. If buyers are to provide this assistance, they should participate in calculating the true cost of the production elements with the vendor. This is very important when one is buying from companies in developing countries or assisting in the development of disadvantaged minority vendors of custom products in the United States.

Another time cost negotiation is important is when products are bought as part of a value analysis or cost reduction program. Value engineering and value analysis are more often discussed than carried out. However, buyers have an obligation to their company to motivate vendors to provide alternative materials that perform the same functions as the higher priced ones. This type of negotiation is a basic part of all purchasing departments' planning for future material shortages.

Certain industries (glass, steel, petrochemicals) use standard price lists to calculate the selling price of their products. The selling prices are often determined independently of the actual cost of producing the product. An industry leader, usually the largest manufacturer, establishes a price list, and the other vendors follow the list in order to remain competitive. Good negotiators are often able to get concessions other than price from "price list" industries. The size of the buyer's company *is not* always the determining factor in whether the vendor will give concessions.

When construction and other labor-intensive contractual services are involved, the calculation of the cost of labor is often negotiable. There are many valid arguments for and against "cost-plus" construction buying. Buyers who are involved in the purchase of labor-intensive services can make significant profit contributions to their companies by carefully negotiating with the vendors.

Another time cost negotiation is important is when the final selling price cannot be determined before completion of the product or project. This situation is very common in research and development buying. When vendors are asked to develop a new product, they often are unable to determine exactly the total amount of labor and materials that will be required. Negotiations for this type of purchase are usually centered around how the vendor will calculate costs and how the buyer will audit the vendor's costs.

There are many other instances in which cost negotiation makes sense. Buyers must evaluate the cost of the purchase against the value of the purchase in order to determine whether or not to use cost negotiation.

The Improvement Curve

Buyers can utilize a mathematical technique to determine what a vendor's selling price should be. This technique is commonly known as an improvement curve or an experience curve calculation. Through the use of such a calculation, buyers can determine if a vendor's quoted selling price is reasonable based on past experience.

Past studies of various industries, primarily in the aerospace field, have shown that repetitive production of a product yields certain efficiencies. As the total production quantity doubles in subsequent production runs, the rate of "improvement" due to the manufacturer's experience can be calculated. The studies have also shown that the rate of improvement generally remains constant over the total life of the product.

Using the improvement curve calculation, a buyer can estimate what the future price of a custom manufactured product should be. Before we look at the calculation, it is important to understand the sources of improvement.

Engineering. The preliminary steps in developing and producing a product generally come from the research and development department. A marketing department notifies engineering that there is a need for a product, and engineering develops it within certain parameters, such as cost, shelf life, performance. The initial development of a product utilizes an engineer's past experience and his or her knowledge of what might work best. The component parts and methods of manufacturing are generally based on the engineer's best knowledge at the time of design. During the life of the product, the engineering department should learn new methods or discover alternative components that will allow for increased efficiency in production and for product improvements. The experience curve measures the degree of implementation of this experience.

Manufacturing. The initial production run of a new product is generally quite inefficient. The workers have to be trained in all facets of making the new product. They can be expected to make mistakes during the early parts of the production run that must be corrected before the product is salable. The workers also must become skilled in the techniques required to produce the product efficiently. Skill development continues throughout the entire life of the product.

Machinery and equipment. New technology, improved machinery, and better types of tooling provide opportunities for more efficient production. As the quantity of the product increases, the manufacturer can afford to invest capital in improved methods and equipment.

Purchasing. Cost reductions due to volume increases, new vendor identification, or the establishment of negotiated contracts are generally available to buyers.

Marketing. In many industries the marketing channels (methods of getting the product from the manufacturer to the customer) are a major cost factor. Improvements in the marketing channels come from experience.

Other areas. There are very few individuals in a company— from top management to first-line laborers—who do not gain experience during the life of a product. The experience curve measures the rate of experience and the speed at which it is implemented.

Improvement Calculations

Studies have proven that once the *rate of improvement* has been calculated for a specific area of a company for a specific product, this rate remains constant over the life of the product. When the rate of improvement is calculated and plotted on a logarithmic curve, it is a straight line over each doubling of the initial quantity of the product (1, 2, 4, 8, 16, . . .). The normal formula for experience is expressed in logarithms. Another formula which will yield the same result is

$$(\%L)^n = \frac{\text{new price}}{\text{original price}}$$

where $\%L$ equals the rate of improvement or experience and n equals the number of times the original quantity has doubled.

To calculate the actual curve with a high degree of accuracy, one must first calculate improvement curves for each area of a business and then calculate the final curve from these individual curves. A buyer using the improvement curve for negotiation planning can use a less exact method to calculate a general curve that will serve as a basis for a negotiation strategy.

CASE STUDY: A buyer has been purchasing a product from a sole source of supply for many years. The vendor's past pricing has had the following pattern:

Year	Contract Quantity	Price	Inflation Rate
1	1000	$800.00	—
2	1000	$792.00	10%
3	2000	$764.64	8%
4	4000	$758.16	12%

The buyer can contract for 8000 pieces in year 5 and has obtained a quotation from the seller of $745/ea based on the buyer's increased quantity and the inflation rate of 10 percent.

Using the improvement curve calculation, the buyer can determine a past pricing "experience" for the vendor. The rate for year 2 is based on increasing the year 1 price by 10 percent and dividing the year 2 price by the inflation-adjusted year 1 price ($792/$880) or 90 percent learning. The year 3 rate is based on increasing the year 1 price by 18 percent (the sum of year 2 and year 3 inflation) and dividing the year 3 price by the inflation-adjusted year 1 price ($764.64/$944.00) and then taking the square root of the answer (.81), since the year 3 price is the second doubling of the original quantity of 1000. The final answer for year 3 would be 90 percent.

The answer for year 4 will also be 90 percent if the reader multiplies the original price by 30 percent and takes the cube root of the answer.

Using improvement curve pricing, the buyer can calculate what the pricing should be for year 5. To perform the calculations properly the buyer must:

1. Multiply the original price by 1.40 to adjust for the total inflation since the original purchase. ($800 × 1.4 = $1120)

2. Calculate the total number of times the original quantity has doubled. The result should be 4.

3. Use the basic formula $(\%L)^n = \dfrac{\text{new price}}{\text{original price}}$ to calculate the new price based on past experience, i.e., 90 percent. The calculation should be as follows:

$$(.9)^4 = \frac{\text{new price}}{\$1120}$$

$$.6561 = \frac{\text{new price}}{\$1120}$$

new price = $734.83

The quotation of $745 is inconsistent with the past pricing methods of the vendor. The buyer can establish a negotiation target price of $734 with confidence. This answers the question of many buyers, "How low can I go?"

The improvement curve can also be used to evaluate the future selling prices of various vendors based on their past experience curve. The following example illustrates an evaluation of three vendors' bids utilizing the experience curve. The example shows that the high bidder, Vendor 1, will actually be the lowest cost vendor in the future.

CASE STUDY: Three vendors bid on a custom fabricated part. The selected vendor will produce the part until it is no longer needed. The selected vendors quoted the following:

Vendor 1: $125/each for 100 parts, 85% historical improvement

Vendor 2: $115/each for 100 parts, 95% historical improvement

Vendor 3: $120/each for 100 parts, 90% historical improvement

Calculate the future unit price up to 5000 pieces using the improvement curve (IC).

$$(\%L)^n = \frac{NP}{OP}; \qquad (\%L)^n \times OP = NP$$

Results are as follows.

Vendor 1: $50.37 ($125 orig. bid), 85% IC
Vendor 2: $86.25 ($115 orig. bid), 95% IC
Vendor 3: $66.48 ($120 orig. bid), 90% IC

Calculation of Multiplier (%L)

Qty	n	1 (85%)	2 (95%)	3 (90%)
100	0			
200	1	.850	.950	.900
400	2	.722	.903	.810
800	3	.614	.857	.729
1600	4	.522	.815	.656
3200	5	.444	.774	.590
5000	5.6	.403	.750	.554

Calculation of Future Price

Qty	1	2	3
100	$125.00	$115.00	$120.00
200	106.25	109.25	108.00
400	90.25	103.84	97.20
800	76.25	98.55	87.48
1600	65.25	93.73	78.72
3200	55.50	89.01	70.80
5000	50.37	86.25	66.48

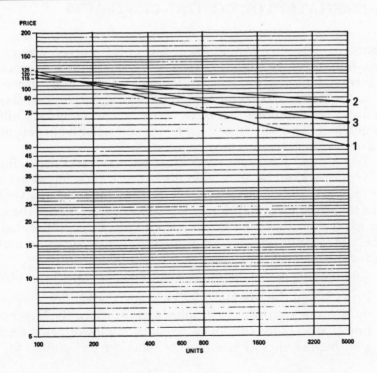

Preparing for Cost Negotiations

Buyers who wish to do cost negotiations must start by analyzing the cost elements of the vendors' products.

Many purchasing departments are adding engineers and cost analysts to their staffs to assist buyers in preparing for cost negotiations. The engineer usually starts by preparing a bill of material listing all the components that go into the final product. There are many price indices available for determining the cost of the elements of a product and for determining a vendor's labor costs. These include trade publications, government statistics, labor contracts, and the vendor's published financial statements. Quite often a buyer can find out a vendor's costs just by asking the vendor.

The amount of time required to prepare for cost negotiations is often considerably longer than that required for price negotiations, but the benefits usually justify the time expended.

RENEGOTIATION OF EXISTING CONTRACTS

Because of changing conditions in the world market, one rarely sees a long-term contract that does not have some provision for the buyer and seller to renegotiate certain terms and conditions before the contract's expiration date. The original contract should establish the conditions that must occur before a contract will be renegotiated. This will protect the buyer and seller from becoming involved in "negotiations to renegotiate."

The scope of renegotiation must be very carefully defined. The vendor should be allowed to discuss only those elements that have changed and created the need for renegotiation. If a vendor wants to discuss all of the elements of the contract before the contract expiration date, the buyer must make a decision either to cancel the contract and negotiate an entirely new agreement or to enforce the original contract.

The reasons for "reopening" a negotiated contract usually are

1. Price. When the market price changes, the vendor may need more money in order to supply the product, or the buyer may find that all other vendors are selling at a lower price. Generally, buyers should use cost negotiation techniques for all

price renegotiations. The price changes allowed should be based on the vendor's actual cost changes, not on the total absorbed costs.

2. Specifications. Changes in item specifications due to government regulations or product liability requirements often lead to contract renegotiation. Provisions for this type of renegotiation should be part of every purchase contract in areas in which the possibility of such changes exists.

3. Quantity. The original contract quantity may increase or decrease. If the quantity increases, the buyer will want to renegotiate the prices in order to take advantage of the larger than expected purchase quantities. Vendors will want to raise prices if the quantity decreases.

ONE-ON-ONE NEGOTIATION

Every time a vendor visits a buyer, some kind of negotiation takes place. The purpose of every sales call is the exchange of information between a buyer and a seller. Buyers should always be prepared for this exchange of information. Many major agreements begin with informal conversations during routine sales calls.

Buyers will often meet with vendors to discuss the terms of future business arrangements. Generally, sellers will prepare for these meetings by analyzing the buyer's past business activity. Too often the buyer does no planning and is not prepared to ask for or respond to vendor concessions. Buyers have an obligation to their companies to prepare for all meetings with vendors. This planning need not involve a great deal of time and effort. The buyer's preparation may just be anticipating the vendor's "real purposes" for visiting the buyer and establishing how to reply to vendor proposals.

Routine sales calls present an excellent opportunity for a buyer to evaluate a seller's receptiveness to future concessions. These meetings can also be used to resolve issues that might create major disagreements if they were discussed in formal negotiation sessions. Informal meetings between key negotiators are often used in labor and government negotiations to resolve conflict.

Sellers will often bring people, including their sales manager, to business meetings with buyers. This is especially likely if the meeting is to discuss the future business relationship. However, this puts the buyer at a psychological disadvantage. The daily relationship of buyer and seller usually establishes them as equals. In bringing along the sales manager, the vendor introduces a person in a superior position to the buyer. A buyer must be very cautious of his or her actions and words when alone with two representatives of a seller's company.

TEAM NEGOTIATION

The use of a negotiating team is recommended for the most formal negotiations. A team provides the buyer with additional resources during the negotiations. The input of the team members during the negotiations will assist the buyer in examining all of the issues and establishing the objectives of the buyer's company. During negotiations, questions may arise that a buyer does not wish to or cannot answer. A properly trained team can provide the buyer with alternatives to giving a direct answer to a vendor's question.

Proper selection of the team members is very important. If there are many divisions in the buyer's company and the buyer is negotiating a contract that will affect several of the divisions, there should be a representative from each of the divisions on the team. The division representatives will be able to introduce issues from their respective divisions. They will also be more receptive to accepting the terms of the contract if they have participated in the original negotiations.

The presence of the chief executive officer at negotiations may be impressive to the seller, but disadvantageous to the buyer's company. If the chief executive agrees to a vendor's offer during the session in front of the seller, the buyer can no longer be effective as the head negotiator. It is recommended that the chief executive join the negotiations only after the buyer and seller have reached agreement.

During team negotiations one person must be designated as the chief spokesperson. This person is usually, but not always, the final decision maker. The final decision maker will function as the team head and will be responsible for controlling the actions of the other members of the negotiating team. In purchasing negotiations, it is very frustrating to have a member of the negotiations team make a statement that is embarrassing to the buyer's company. A good team leader will establish the team members' roles before the start of negotiations and thus prevent such occurrences.

INTERNATIONAL NEGOTIATION

The entire world is the marketplace for materials and services. It is becoming increasingly common for buyers to seek out vendors from different countries. Negotiating with these vendors introduces problems that are not common in the buyer's own country.

The first rule of international negotiation is never to tell vendors that they are *foreign*. Vendors are only foreign when in the buyer's country. Buyers are foreign when in the vendor's country.

International negotiation brings together people with different cultural backgrounds and customs. Buyers should attempt to understand the vendors' customs and methods of doing business before negotiating with them. This understanding will help ensure that the contract which is negotiated can be implemented.

Every person has some prejudices. Buyers must be very careful to overcome any prejudices about a seller's country. These prejudices can subconsciously affect the buyer's ability to be effective. Courtesy and respect for the seller's position are very important in international negotiation. "Saving face" is a concept that buyers must understand in order to negotiate with persons from any culture.

Another important factor that buyers must understand is that English is not the common language of the rest of the world. It is often advantageous to negotiate with interpreters in order to ensure that the negotiating parties fully understand one another. If interpreters are used, the buyer should never use interpreters furnished by the seller. That would be tantamount to using a seller as part of the buyer's negotiating team.

A major problem many buyers have to face in international negotiations is the seller's concept of time. Buyers who are under pressure to complete a negotiation may have to make concessions that they would not have made if they had had more time to negotiate. Many vendors take advantage of a buyer's time constraints by discussing major negotiation issues only when the buyer is under time pressure.

The attitude of vendors in developing countries toward doing business is sometimes very passive. Buyer's may find that the seller's attitude toward on-time delivery or highly sophisticated specifications is somewhat less exacting than the buyer is accustomed to in his or her own country. These attitudes must be taken into consideration if the buyer is to be satisfied with the contract.

The selling terms of international business agreements are also different. The use of special banking and legal resources is often required to support the final negotiation.

A key factor to remember for all international negotiations is that there are very few items that are not negotiable, from the original specifications to the currency of payment to the ship that carries the final delivery. A lack of thorough preparation for international negotiations can be far more costly than a lack of preparation for domestic negotiations.

SUMMARY

Not all negotiations are the same. The amount of preparation needed depends on the type of negotiation the buyer is involved in. Buyers must recognize, before negotiations start, what type of negotiation is going to take place and the advantages and disadvantages of that type of negotiation. This recognition will ensure success.

Price negotiations are the most basic type of negotiation; they require the least amount of planning and should probably be considered the minimum for most routine purchases. Buyers who routinely ask for concessions in exchange for business will find that their costs will consistently decline or stabilize.

Cost negotiations can be a major contribution to assuring that buyers are optimizing their vendors' resources. Increased use of cost negotiations has the potential of changing a buyer-supplier relationship from an adversary one in which there is great mistrust between the parties to a contractor-subcontractor one in which the vendor becomes an extension of the buyer's company. Closer vendor relationships will become critical in future years.

The utilization of improvement curve calculations, based on proven mathematical techniques, can be a major factor in controlling future costs. The use of these quantitative methods should be standard practice in every professional purchasing department. An expanded discussion of these techniques can be found in the National Association of Purchasing Management's *Guide to Purchasing*, Section 1.13, "The Improvement Curve Technique," by Charles H. Adams, Rockwell International Corporation.

One-on-one negotiations, a meeting between a buyer and a seller, should occur in some form every time a buyer meets with a salesperson. The purpose of all meetings is to exchange information.

Low-value negotiations are usually one-on-one. But the absence of a negotiating team does not eliminate a buyer's need to plan for the meeting. Often one-on-one negotiations are the most difficult kind of negotiation because buyers do not have additional resources available during the negotiation. Buyers should try to avoid negotiating alone when a vendor arrives at a negotiating session with more than one person.

Team negotiation, the technique used for most labor and government negotiations, is recommended for formal negotiations. It works very well in purchasing. Leveraging a buyer's skills with those of other experts can be a major factor in negotiation success.

International negotiation requires considerably more planning than domestic negotiation. As international trade increases, buyers must become more aware of the differing business considerations of various countries. With international vendors the negotiable items are often considerably broader than with domestic vendors. Enforcement of international contracts is difficult unless they are carefully negotiated and documented.

A combination of negotiation types is required in certain situations. For example, if the vendor is from another country and the commodity being negotiated represents a major custom-produced product, cost negotiation, team negotiation, and international negotiation are involved. Buyers should be familiar with the different types of negotiations and be flexible enough to use those that provide the most leverage.

3

Determining
What Is Negotiable

In order to negotiate effectively, buyers must understand the various factors to be considered when they are planning for negotiations. These factors will become the issues to be resolved during the actual negotiations. Discussion and resolution of the items will ensure a workable contract; too often issues that are not discussed create problems during contract implementation.

This chapter has been divided into five major sections:

1. Major issues for all negotiations,
2. Construction and contractual service contracts,
3. Machinery and equipment contracts,
4. Inventory for resale,
5. Maintenance, repair, and operational supplies (MRO) contracts.

Each section will discuss the various factors that buyers should consider before entering into negotiations with vendors. The discussion will also delve into issues involving various types of commodities. It is impossible to discuss every commodity in a book this size. We apologize, in advance, to any reader whose commodity was overlooked.

MAJOR ISSUES FOR ALL NEGOTIATIONS

All negotiations, regardless of commodity, cover certain major issues. These issues must be resolved before any agreement can be reached. For certain minor types of purchases, these issues can be the basis of the contract. However, for major purchases, these issues are only a part of the contract.

Almost every industry has *price* customs. Buyers must remember that these customs were developed by the industry to protect the seller. Good negotiators negotiate around industry customs. If buyers can negotiate in a manner different from other buyers, they can usually achieve some very favorable price concessions. For instance, truck transportation rates are normally based on a certain price per hundred pounds for specific commodities. However, the cost of moving a loaded truck one mile can be calculated fairly easily. Buyers who negotiate transportation on a cost per mile basis may achieve some surprising savings.

Competition is often the major factor affecting a vendor's willingness to negotiate. Buyers are not obligated to disclose what other vendors quote (except for government buying). Buyers can take advantage of a seller's concern about the competition to negotiate a lower price. However, buyers who establish artificially low "quotes" in order to get a vendor to lower a price are violating laws and may be prosecuted.

The buyer's volume of purchase will always be an important factor in the seller's decision to lower a price. Buyers should be able to discuss various volume levels when negotiating. These various levels are produced when buyers allocate different percentages of their business to specific vendors or when they negotiate contracts for longer terms. The buyer can also use the time length of the contract to gain concessions.

The past relationship of the buyer and seller will often affect the seller's willingness to negotiate price. If the buyer has never negotiated in the past, the seller is often very surprised when the buyer begins negotiating. Many buyers know their vendors so well that they assume that a vendor is giving them the best prices without negotiation. When a buyer presumes to know everything there is to know about a vendor, it is time to change buyers.

The rising costs due to inflation in recent years have prevented many vendors from providing long-term, fixed price contracts. Buyers can negotiate how and under what circumstances prices will be revised. Future price increases often cost less than long-term fixed prices based on estimates of what prices will be in the future. Price escalations should be based on specific events that can be independently evaluated by the buyer in the marketplace. These events must be described in the purchase contract, and the vendor must prove that they have occurred before being allowed to increase prices.

The events that affect the selling price should relate to the vendor's *direct* costs of materials and labor. Buyers should attempt to negotiate that prices increase by the actual costs, not by the additives of overhead, general and administrative expenses, and profits. The discussion in Chapter 2 of cost negotiation illustrated the impact of these additives.

Any purchase agreement that allows a vendor to increase prices because of changing costs should also have a provision to decrease prices.

The cost of money (interest rates) has a direct effect on selling prices. Payment terms that are extended or that provide for a discount for early payment are equivalent to a price reduction. However, buyers should be on the lookout for discounts that, if taken, actually cost more than delaying payment until the final due date. Before accepting a discount the buyer should check with his or her finance department to affirm that the discount is really advantageous.

Whether the buyer or seller pays for transportation will affect the final delivered price. Possible methods of transportation and the cost of each method must also be considered. Buyers can often transport materials more cheaply than sellers. These alternatives can be very profitable.

There are many selling terms such as FOB shipping point, FOB delivered, freight-alongside-ship, or cost of insurance and freight (title transfers at vendor's ship but vendor pays freight). These terms affect where the title to the purchased goods transfers. Many times the vendor will pay for the freight but transfer the title to the materials to the buyer long before the materials are received. Loss or damage to materials thus becomes the buyer's responsibility and problem. If the title was transferred before the buyer received the goods, the buyer is also obligated to pay the full sales price of even lost or damaged goods to the seller. The buyer should evaluate the chances of loss or damage and the probable costs of resolving such losses before a final agreement on selling terms is reached.

In international purchasing, the payment terms, often based on a specified event such as transfer at a port or clearance through customs, can be documented in a letter of credit issued by the buyer's bank. The occurrence of the event authorizes the buyer's bank to transfer the purchase price to the seller's bank account.

The event can occur independently of actions of the buyer, so the buyer may find that he or she has paid for unwanted materials. This happens most often when the letter of credit states that the seller can receive payment upon presentation of a bill of lading proving the shipment has been made.

Payment terms of letters of credit can be negotiated. Before final agreement is reached in any purchase that requires a letter of credit, the buyer should make sure he or she understands the terms of the letter of credit and the implications of the terms for the buyer's company.

Price is too often considered the only issue to be negotiated. In many purchases the price may be the least important issue, particularly when there are limited sources of supply or when quality is the major determinant of price.

Services provided by sellers often reduce the total cost of buying a product or service and can be a major issue for negotiation.

On-time delivery is the most desirable service any vendor can provide to a buyer, yet it is often the most difficult one to receive. Many buyers would be willing to make major concessions to sellers in order to be guaranteed 100 percent on-time delivery. Buyers can negotiate to obtain on-time delivery. To do this, buyers must understand the seller's business methods and analyze the elements that are required in order for on-time delivery to occur.

The factors that affect a vendor's ability to deliver on time include:

1. The amount of time the vendor needs to enter the buyer's order into the vendor's system,
2. The availability of materials needed to fill the buyer's order,
3. The availability of qualified labor to work on the buyer's order,
4. The available capacity of any machinery and equipment required,
5. The standard production time required to produce the order,
6. The available transportation,
7. The documentation requirements, and
8. The inspection requirements.

Since most vendors have many customers, buyers must compete for fast service. Buyers can negotiate each of the above factors and determine what bottlenecks might affect the seller's ability to perform on time. Many buyers provide resources to their vendors to assist them in achieving on-time delivery. These resources range from automated order entry systems to raw materials or transportation.

Many vendors are willing to warehouse raw materials or finished products for buyers who make a firm commitment to accept the materials. This commitment gives the vendor the resources to provide service to the buyer and should reduce the purchase price.

Several large companies are involving vendors in their master scheduling programs. This allows vendors to receive long-range plans of the buyer and thus better support the buyer's needs. This involvement often includes special computer hookups between buyers and sellers to speed the transmission of information. These systems also eliminate a great deal of paperwork.

Buyers who are buying many different items which are produced by a similar process may consider making a commitment for a percentage of a vendor's available capacity. If the commitment for capacity is spread over the life of the contract as a fixed number of hours per day, week, or month, the buyers can reduce lead time and increase flexibility for last-minute changes. However, the disadvantage of buying capacity is that the buyer usually pays the vendor for any unused capacity that the vendor cannot resell elsewhere.

Quality materials and *workmanship* are the overriding factors of any purchase. If the quality is unacceptable, the lowest price and best service become meaningless. What is acceptable is often not clearly defined. Many contract disputes arise when the buyer and seller disagree about what they negotiated to be acceptable quality. Before negotiations are completed, both buyer and seller should agree fully on functional and visual standards. They should establish the rules for acceptance and rejection of an order and the consequences of rejection.

Inspection procedures performed by the buyer and seller vary according to type of purchase. If quality standards are agreed on in advance, vendors can provide inspection services that historically have been performed by buyers. When sellers perform the inspection procedures, they must verify that the inspection has been performed and that the purchased items conformed. Vendors must also accept *full* responsibility for nonperformance. This responsibility may exceed the cost of the purchase. If it does, the limits of liability must be a part of the original contract. The vendor's responsibility for replacing defective products or services must also be clearly defined. The buyer's company will need replacements promptly and should not have to wait the vendor's "normal" lead time.

The terms of *warranties* for purchase of certain items or labor are also negotiable. Standard warranties often do not offer the buyer's organization adequate protection. A special warranty may increase the cost of a purchase, but its benefits may justify the additional cost.

Contract terms and conditions vary from very complex to very simple, depending on the nature of the purchase. All purchase agreements should be considered a contract between a buyer and a seller. Chapter 6 discusses the various legal pitfalls that the buyer should avoid.

Enforcement of the contract in courts may become an issue. The buyer should have full vendor agreement on exactly which courts have final jurisdiction if it becomes necessary to take a contract to a court. This is especially important for international purchases.

It should be hoped that the contract will not have to be cancelled. Cancellation indicates that both buyer and seller failed. However, every contract should specify the methods of cancellation and the buyer's and seller's rights if the contract is cancelled.

If possible, the buyer should never sign a vendor's contract. Buyers should prepare contracts on forms approved by their own legal department to be assured of the greatest protection. Buyers should be aware of any "standard" paragraphs in a vendor's contract that might be controversial. One indication that a buyer should examine a vendor's contract is if the vendor replies, "No problem," when the buyer questions the terms. This reply should alert the buyer to the need for greater examination of the contract. Any issue that is not documented in a contract is a potential problem.

CONSTRUCTION AND CONTRACTUAL SERVICE CONTRACTS

Construction and contractual service vendors normally make their profits through a markup on their labor costs, their subcontractors' costs, and the cost of purchased materials and equipment they install. The skill and experience of the contractor's employees, and the contractor's ability to complete a project on time, are the contractor's major selling points. Factors affecting labor performance, project completion, and warranties of workmanship and equipment are usually major items for negotiation.

Past experience shows that very few construction projects end up exactly the way they started. During the course of the construction, the buyer makes changes to enhance the construction or to alter the scope of the project. These changes can often result in major profit increases for the seller unless the buyer negotiates, in advance, exactly how changes will be priced. Some contractors depend on the changes, or "extras," to make up for the low profit or lack of profit on the original bid.

The types of vendors that sell construction and contractual services include:

1. *Specialty contractors.* Specialty contractors are vendors who restrict the scope of their work to one specialty such as electrical installation or concrete work. These contractors range in size from a company with a few highly skilled craftspersons to the very large companies. These vendors contract with a buyer for a specific job or act as a subcontractor for a major project.

2. *General contractors.* These vendors are responsible for bringing together many skills in order to complete a project. A general contractor may be a company with engineering skills which employs a variety of specialty contractors or a multinational company with large staffs of engineers and craftspersons. The large general contractors also employ specialty contractors to supplement their own labor forces.

3. *Service divisions of machinery and equipment vendors.* Manufacturers and other sellers of capital equipment usually establish service divisions so their customers can call on them for repair and maintenance. Many of these vendors offer service contracts to their customers when they sell their equipment. The profits on these service contracts can be greater than the profits on the sale of the equipment. These vendors also make profits on labor costs and on the sale of replacement parts. Many specialty contractors have gone into competition with service division vendors, so buyers should carefully evaluate both types of vendors before contracting for service.

Negotiating Construction Contracts

A construction contract may range in price from a few thousand dollars to many hundreds of millions of dollars. The buyer may negotiate to pay a fixed price for the project or to pay the contractor's actual cost plus a markup for labor, overhead, materials, and profit. Escalation provisions to accommodate for increased labor and material costs may be a part of both types of contracts. Which type of contract is more suitable depends on how well the buyer can define the scope of the project, the size of the project, the nature of the work, and the buyer's ability to measure the ongoing competence of the contractor during the construction (project management). Many companies have established policies about which type of contract they prefer.

All construction negotiations should resolve certain issues. Resolution and documentation of these issues will prevent many problems.

The *type of labor* used by the contractor must be defined. Many companies must use only unionized contractor labor. If nonunion labor is brought onto a property with union labor, a major problem can be created. Certain countries require that nationals of their country be used wherever possible. If a contractor attempts to import labor, the government may shut the construction project down. In construction projects for United States government agencies, normally disadvantaged minority workers must comprise a certain percentage of the labor force.

The contractor must *warrant* the quality of workmanship and the operability of installed machinery and equipment. All factors involving the contractor's warranty are negotiable. The scope of the warranty will generally extend beyond final payment for the project, so the kinds of recourse available to the vendor and buyer if the warranty is violated should be defined.

The contractor must have *rights of access* to the buyer's property in order to complete the work. The buyer may require that the vendor restrict access to only the construction site and limit staff to only required personnel in order to improve the buyer's security. Many buyers will provide materials to contractors, but access to the buyer's supply rooms should not be granted to the contractor.

Special *facilities* will often be needed for the contractor's project management staff and for storage of materials. The extent and location of these facilities should be defined. Who pays for the cost of these facilities should also be defined.

Insurance coverage and extent of liability must be defined. If a contractor's employee is injured anywhere on the buyer's property, the buyer may be liable unless the insurance issue was resolved previously. Insurance should cover contractor labor, vehicles, equipment, and facilities. The coverage should also handle contractor damage to any of the buyer's properties, facilities, or employees. The amount of liability must be sufficient to cover major mishaps. No construction work should start before the vendor has furnished a certificate of liability from an insurance company acceptable to the buyer. Many buyers have pointed out that small contractors are unable to provide the required insurance. In these cases, the buyer's company may wish to provide the insurance to the contractor through its insurance carrier.

Progress reports on the percentage of work completed should be the contractor's responsibility. Often payment is based on this percentage. What is meant by "complete" should be negotiated and resolved. The buyer should be able to verify a vendor's report on completion or percentage of completion.

The *extent of the contractor's services* must be clearly defined in the original contract. The responsibilities of the contractor and the buyer's companies may vary. When the contractor assumes additional responsibilities during a project, the cost is usually very high.

Engineering changes during a construction project are not unusual. The contract should very clearly define who has the authority to request and approve changes, how the changes are to be documented, and how the contractor will calculate the charges for the changes. Unless this is done before the project begins, the final cost may be considerably higher than the original estimate and the contractor may have a free hand to charge exorbitant costs for changes.

If the original contract allows the contractor to increase charges because of *escalation of labor and material costs,* the contract should define exactly how the contractor will calculate these costs. It should also require that the contractor provide documentation of the cost escalation to the buyer. The contract may restrict the amount of escalation to a certain percentage or limit the contractor's ability to escalate prices to specified time periods.

Licenses and permits are required for most construction projects. These licenses and permits usually must be purchased from local governments to ensure that the work complies with local regulations. Normally the contractor is responsible for purchasing them, but the buyer may be liable if the contract does not specify responsibility. If the proper licenses and permits are not obtained before construction is started, the project may be stopped or delayed for significant periods and heavy fines may be assessed. The buyer and vendor must agree on who is responsible for the cost of delay and fines due to lack of the proper permits.

The *working hours* of the contractor may conflict with the buyer's working hours, particularly if the contractor is working inside a buyer's existing structure. If a contractor is working a seven-day week, the buyer must also resolve the issue of overtime payments to the contractor's labor force.

Another point for negotiation is when the *title of equipment* is transferred. When equipment is installed or furnished by the contractor, the title may not transfer until the equipment is operating to the buyer's satisfaction, or it may transfer before the equipment is ever installed.

The original manufacturer may specify certain installation requirements and operating parameters. *Equipment warranties* may be voided if the contractor modifies the equipment. The contract should clarify who is responsible for a warranty if the contractor violates these requirements.

If a *patent infringement* occurs in installed contractor equipment, the buyer may be liable to the infringed company. The contract should protect the buyer from third-party claims.

Many buyers require *start-up assistance* with installed equipment. The contract should define the extent of this assistance and whether it is included in the total contract price.

Responsibility for cleaning up the construction site at the end of the project should also belong to the contractor.

Force majeure is a clause protecting the contractor from defaults in completion due to riots, strikes, etc. The contract should define this clause, too.

Liens on the construction may be assessed by subcontractors who have not been paid by the contractor. The final contract should have a provision to protect the buyer from these liens.

The buyer should define the vendor's *right to assign* the contract or subcontract work to another company.

Fixed price contract negotiations should also define:

1. Everything included and not included in the fixed price,
2. Extra charges caused by delays made by the buyer,
3. Incentives or penalties for early or late completion.

Cost-plus contract negotiations should resolve:

1. All cost elements for labor rates of pay, including overtime,
2. Methods of charging overhead and administration,
3. Costs for tools and small equipment,
4. Markup of purchased items,
5. Contractor minimum and maximum profit allowances,
6. Labor productivity,
7. Buyer's rights to audit vendor's records.

Negotiating Service Agreements

Buyers who purchase maintenance services from vendors can negotiate the extent and types of services to be performed. These agreements generally fall into two major categories: the routine maintenance of equipment for a specified period and special maintenance services.

Routine maintenance may be purchased from the equipment manufacturer or from a specialty contractor. The buyers should make sure that they understand the exact scope of the work to be performed by the vendor. Often service contracts do not include costs of certain spare parts or special types of repairs. The buyer must also make sure that there is a way to tell whether maintenance services were actually performed according to the contract specifications. Maintenance service negotiations should also define how often the vendor will perform routine preventative maintenance. If emergency maintenance is anticipated, the contract should define whether or not this is included.

If the service agreement is for warranty work on equipment, the buyer and seller should clearly understand the extent of work the buyer is allowed to perform on the equipment without voiding the warranty. The location of warranty work must also be defined. Many a vendor will do warranty work only at the vendor's location; the buyer must transport the item to be worked on to the seller at the buyer's expense.

Before agreeing to pay for routine service for a new machine, buyers should carefully examine the warranty provided as part of the initial purchase to ensure that the warranty does not provide for the same services at no charge. This will prevent buyers from paying for the same services twice, first in the initial purchase price and then in the charge for the service agreement.

An alternative to purchasing routine maintenance services from the original manufacturer may be to buy these services from an independent company that specializes in maintenance services and costs less. If the services are performed by qualified mechanics, the warranty may not be voided.

The use of a *loaner* piece of equipment can often be negotiated as part of the service agreement. The loaner is available to the buyer at no fee or for a very low cost. This must be agreed on before the agreement is signed, not when the loaner is needed.

CAPITAL MACHINERY AND EQUIPMENT

Capital machinery and equipment includes all acquisitions that have a useful life of over one year and that exceed a certain unit value preestablished by the organization. These acquisitions often require a capital appropriation approval. The only exception is construction, which was discussed in the previous section.

Machinery falls into three major categories:

1. *Standard.* The seller provides exactly the same piece of machinery or equipment to every customer without options or accessories. This category includes typewriters, office machines, and some production machinery.

2. *Customized.* The seller customizes a standard model of a machine to fit a customer's specific needs. Normally the customization relates to options (features that *must be selected* in order for the machine to operate, such as a motor and transmission) or accessories (features that *may be selected* to enhance the machine, such as air conditioning or a radio).

3. *Custom-built.* The seller builds a machine to satisfy a need of a specific customer. The machine may be composed of standard parts such as a motor or electrical control, but the overall design and construction of the machine is customized.

The final selection of a capital equipment vendor is normally made jointly by purchasing and the end user of the equipment. It is often more cost-effective to standardize the type of machines purchased over a period of time than to always purchase the machine with the lowest cost. The life cycle cost of equipment, which includes maintenance, spare parts, and operating efficiency, is often more important than the initial purchase price. Standardized equipment allows the buyer's company to reduce the total cost of owning the equipment.

Normally, equipment is purchased to satisfy a specific need. If performance specifications are needed, the buyer can often negotiate with the vendor for equipment that will meet the specifications. If the equipment fails to perform as promised, the buyer's company has recourse.

Many companies buy only custom-built machinery. Buyers have a responsibility to their companies to evaluate other vendors of standard and customized machinery to determine if alternatives to the custom-built machines exist. The machinery and equipment industries are constantly introducing new equipment that may perform as well as the custom-built equipment of the past. Cost negotiations should be used whenever possible for costly custom-built machines.

Performance is probably the major negotiating objective for all machinery. If the machine does not perform to expectations, it is useless. The buyer should understand exactly what can be expected from the machine and what the vendor will do if the machine fails to perform as expected.

The *installation, start-up, and training assistance* provided by the vendor will be a factor in how fast the buyer's company will be able to use the equipment productively. Many vendors will provide this assistance as part of the original cost. The amount of assistance is often limited to a certain number of days. Buyers can negotiate for a longer period of assistance if they feel that the vendor does not offer adequate time.

Machinery installation assistance by the seller is often contingent upon the buyer's moving the equipment to its final location. The buyer is also usually responsible for air, water, electricity, or gas hookups to the machine. Delays caused by the buyer's failure to provide the lines can void the vendor's obligation to provide assistance. These issues should be clearly understood before the contract is signed.

Electrical, air, or gas specifications may be unique to the buyer's company or country. This is particularly true for electrical specifications, which include the voltage and machinery cycles. Many parts of the world operate on 220-volt, 50-cycle electricity for household power, while the United States and Canada operate on 110-volt, 60-cycle electricity. The electrical specifications for imported machinery should be carefully agreed on and documented. The type of gas used in machines with heating units can be natural or liquid petroleum gas; these specifications should also be documented.

Equipment blueprints and specifications are not always made available by the equipment manufacturer. Buyers have a better chance of obtaining these specifications if they request them during negotiations.

Government regulations (OSHA, FDA, etc.) often require specific modifications to equipment. If special regulations affect the equipment, responsibility for conformance can often be shifted to the vendor. The negotiations should include what the buyer's recourse is if the machine fails to meet the regulations.

Prepayment and final payment schedules are negotiable. Many vendors request a prepayment with the order and a series of payments during the construction of the equipment. This is particularly true for custom-built equipment. The final payment should not be made until the buyer is satisfied that the machine has been correctly installed and is working at the performance level expected.

Spare parts should be available for the life of the equipment. Often spare parts can be purchased from local vendors rather than from the manufacturer. The buyer's authority to buy spare parts locally without voiding the warranty must often be negotiated in advance of the purchase.

Vendor maintenance service should be available for the warranty period. The extent and costs of this service should be clearly understood. The buyer's options if the vendor does not provide service within a *reasonable amount of time* must be defined. These options should allow the buyer to obtain service from another source without voiding the warranty. The exact *warranty* and all of its provisions should be clear. Warranty conditions may be negotiated. Buyers should clearly understand various regional and federal laws affecting warranties. Often these regulations require that the vendors warrant more than their warranties state.

The *delivery date* should be the date the equipment is delivered and installed in the buyer's facility, not the date it is shipped from the vendor's facility. Any penalty charges for late delivery should be based on this date.

Vendors often charge extra for *packing or crating* a machine. When title transfers at the point of shipment, buyers may wish to obtain special types of packing to ensure that the chances of damage are minimized.

Freight, insurance, and other transportation and transfer charges can have a major impact on the total cost of the purchase. The negotiations should define who is responsible for these charges and the method of transportation to be used during the shipment.

The negotiations should also define who is responsible for *import custom duties and licenses* which may be required. The charges negotiated should include those made by a customs broker.

Of course, *price* is the final point of agreement. Often the price will be determined automatically by adding up the costs of all the factors already discussed. Buyers must remember that there are very few pieces of machinery or equipment that are sold at the list price.

INVENTORY FOR RESALE

We are defining inventory as those classes of purchases that are used as part of a product for resale in manufacturing, wholesaling, distribution, and retailing. Purchases of items consumed by organizations (banks, insurance companies, manufacturing, etc.) will be discussed in the next section.

Since considerations are somewhat different for the various

types of inventory, this section has been divided into six major parts:

1. Negotiations for all types of inventory,
2. Price list industry negotiations,
3. Fabricated wood, metal, and plastic negotiations,
4. Printing (including paper and paperboard packaging) negotiations,
5. Electronic component and subassembly negotiations,
6. Contract assembly and contract packaging negotiations.

For companies that resell the inventory as their product, the cost of owning inventory can exceed 30 percent of the cost of the inventory per year. Therefore, the purchasing department should be highly skilled in this facet of buying. The opportunities for negotiating on inventory purchases are better than those in any other area of purchasing because of the repetitive nature of the purchasing and the relatively high value of the total volume of purchases.

Many buyers are starting to look at their vendors as subcontractors or the buyer's outside manufacturing facilities. The purchase of inventory can be considered to be the purchase of the manufacturing capacity for the product desired. The vendor that can provide the most qualified capacity (quality and service) at the lowest cost will normally get the order. Negotiations should revolve around "qualified capacity" and cost.

Negotiations for All Types of Inventory

Reduction or *stabilization of cost* is the most talked about objective for inventory negotiating. This concern is well deserved, since the profits of the buyer's organization are based on markups on costs of labor and materials, and material costs often comprise 80 percent of the direct costs. Buyers should always assume that vendors are willing to discuss cost concessions, no matter how small the buyer's volume.

Reducing inventory investment through the negotiation of smaller delivery quantities is often equivalent to a price reduction. The purchase of reduced quantities will improve inventory turnover and allow the buyer's company to pursue other investments.

Assurance of inventory supply during periods of shortage may be very important. Buyers who remember periods of materials shortages in past years should be willing to develop negotiation strategies to ensure supply. The buyer's company should have sufficient flexibility to be able to react to changing market conditions.

Buyers can negotiate for *extended payment terms* which permit the company to recover the cost of purchased inventory in the same period in which payment is made. This is often an excellent alternative to borrowing money to finance the purchase of inventory.

Quality is negotiable! Too many buyers do not utilize quality negotiations properly. Quality can be a major factor in determining the overall cost of inventory.

Industry standards concerning quality and quantities of production overruns and underruns have been developed by many industries. These standards should be used only as guidelines; changes to standards can be negotiated. Although many warranties are based on these industry standards, buyers who take the time to negotiate warranties often receive concessions from their vendors.

Price List Industry Negotiations

Certain commodities such as base metals (gold, silver, etc.), agricultural products, or crude oil have published world market prices. These prices are generally established by commodity exchanges or sales cartels such as OPEC. However, investigation shows that large purchasers of these commodities often pay different prices from those published. The published price ends up being the justification for the selling price of products that are based on these commodities—gasoline, chemicals, electronic components, etc.

Since *price* is based on a standard list, many buyers hesitate to negotiate price with these vendors. However, through creative planning the buyer may develop a method of purchasing these items which differs from the industry "standard" and thus achieve price concessions. One good way to achieve price concessions is to ask for *packaging* that differs from industry standards. *Timing* can also be important. During periods of oversupply, many price list industries offer special discounts to entice buyers. Negotiations for price should be directed toward obtaining these discounts.

Another method for obtaining lower prices is to negotiate for the right to *spot buy*. Negotiations should cover the buyer's right to make spot purchases of a certain percentage of contract requirements. Negotiations with distributors of price list commodities should cover the passing on of spot purchase savings to the buyer.

Special long-term contracts that protect buyers against price increases are gaining wide acceptance. Buyers should be careful that the contracts base pricing on an index, such as the producer price index, that can be evaluated independently of the industry price list.

Total usage pricing that is based on the buyer's total contract usage rather than on the release quantity at time of shipment is another alternative to list pricing.

Changes in specifications that make items nonstandard can have a major effect on the price. This is particularly applicable to brand-name items. Manufacturers of brand-name items will often produce a buyer's private brand-name products for considerably less than their own brand-name products.

Allocations of critical materials during periods of shortages often occur in many basic industries, including price list industries. Allocation negotiations are always possible with these industries.

Consignment of inventory at the list price, meaning that it is paid for after the month of actual usage, is often an alternative to price reduction. *Warehousing* by the vendor until materials are shipped to a buyer's location can serve the same function as consignment of inventory, except the vendor assumes the responsibility of storage. Warehousing negotiations should include whether selling price is determined at the time materials enter the vendor's warehouse or at the vendor's time of shipment. Vendor-supplied *storage facilities* and *handling equipment* are offered by many vendors who will not make price concessions. These facilities and equipment can often be obtained in exchange for a long-term agreement.

Fabricated Wood, Metal, and Plastic Negotiations

There are many opportunities for negotiation in the purchase of fabricated parts. Since parts are normally fabricated to meet buyer specifications, there are no standard list prices for these items. Quotation requests can show wide variances in selling prices. Negotiations are almost always beneficial.

Cost negotiations are often required and can cover most of the elements that comprise the selling price. Analytical buyers will identify the key cost elements.

Raw materials specifications and cost can be major factors in the selling price. Raw materials are often purchased from price list industries, so their cost can be determined from published price lists. Slight changes in specifications can have a major effect on the final selling price. The selling price should be based on the raw material cost on the date of the vendor's acquisition of the raw materials, not on the date of shipment to the buyer. Many buyers find that they can supply raw materials to vendors at a cost lower than what the vendor can get elsewhere. Thus, the responsibility for purchase of raw materials can be negotiated.

Tooling to fabricate or produce parts is usually a one-time charge. Tooling may be supplied by either the vendor or the buyer. Buyers should evaluate the options of buying different quality or size tools. This decision will directly affect the quantity of parts the vendor will be able to produce and, in turn, the selling price of the parts purchased. If the vendor supplies the tooling and the buyer pays a separate charge for the tools, the contract should clearly specify the ownership of the tools and the buyer's right to remove the tools in the case of a contract cancellation. If the tooling charge is included in the buyer's per-piece price, the exact tooling charge should be defined so that the buyer does not continue to pay for the tooling after the vendor has recovered costs. *Responsibility for tooling maintenance* should also be defined. Annual routine maintenance charges should not be allowed unless the vendor clearly states what is included.

Quality standards, including performance of parts assembled into the buyer's products, are negotiable. These standards can include definition of the vendor's liability if a part fails because it is substandard.

Vendor's production methods and capacity allocation to the buyer's company directly affect how well the vendor can provide parts when needed to the buyer. Buyers may want to negotiate for a specific percentage of a vendor's capacity on certain machines to ensure availability of completed parts.

Warehousing in the vendor's plants of specified quantities of raw materials, work in process, and finished goods is possible. This allows vendors to respond quickly to changes by buyers in requirements. Such a warehousing agreement usually requires the buyer to be responsible for unused materials at the end of the contract. The buyer's liability for raw materials and work in process is of course much less than the buyer's liability for finished goods.

Printing (Including Paper and Paperboard Packaging) Negotiations

All organizations buy printing. They buy the printing either as an inventory purchase or as part of their operations supplies in the form of promotional materials and forms.

Printing vendors range in size from very small independent companies which use very simple equipment to very large multinational companies which can supply everything from paper to bound books. Selection of the proper vendor through careful quotation and negotiation procedures is very important. *Cost negotiation* possibilities abound in the printing industry. The printing industry example in Chapter 2 illustrated some of the alternatives a buyer may wish to consider.

Formula pricing is a common technique used by high-volume printing buyers to determine the vendor's selling prices for new items. The buyer and seller negotiate an annual pricing formula based on the vendor's costs for materials and labor. The variable costs of price list items such as paper and chemical coatings are often determined through an industry publication such as *The Yellow Sheet* (a weekly publication of raw paper pricing).

Requirements in the areas of *paper weight and quality* can account for up to 70 percent of the selling price. Various types of paper are available to buyers. Often there can be a great difference in price between two paper items with very minor quality differences.

Color variations, particularly in packaging, can cause a buyer's company many problems. Negotiations should include agreement on the acceptable range of color, if this is important.

Warehousing of completed work or of raw paper is quite common in the industry. Both the quantity of items and the length of time they will be warehoused are negotiable.

Preparatory costs for printing plates, dies, and film to make plates are often quoted as extra costs. Buyers can negotiate these preparatory costs and should consider supplying these materials to the vendor.

Paper can be supplied by either the buyer or the vendor. If the buyer supplies the paper, he or she must assume certain risks for loss if the paper does not perform as expected, or if the paper is damaged by the printer during the printing process. The amount of risk to be assumed by the buyer and seller can be resolved through negotiation.

Performance of automated machinery that folds, glues, or otherwise handles paper and packaging can be a major objective for a buyer. The extent of performance and the buyer's options and rights in the case of performance failure should be clearly defined. Many machinery manufacturers license certain vendors to produce packaging to operate on their machinery. If an unlicensed vendor is used, the buyer may be liable for patent infringements and the machinery manufacturer may void the warranty.

Security of printed materials is often an important buyer objective. This is particularly true when one is buying negotiable documents such as checks, lottery tickets or promotional game cards, and promotional packaging. Negotiations about the nature and extent of security are not uncommon.

Coatings and other packaging materials may have to satisfy certain *health or safety performance requirements*, particularly for foods and pharmaceuticals. Often special certification is required from the vendor. This should be agreed upon in advance. A representative of the buyer should have the *right to inspect a vendor's facilities* as part of the conformance requirements.

Drop shipment of materials to many of the buyer's locations can often be arranged. The printer may be required to provide the buyer with either proof of shipment or proof of delivery in order to receive payment.

National contracts for uniform pricing of production at all of a vendor's plants can be negotiated. During this type of negotiation, buyers should make sure that the vendor representative actually has the authority to commit the entire company.

Electronic Component and Subassembly Negotiations

The electronics industry is very volatile, with rapid changes in technology development, wide ranges in quality level for the same component, and decreasing prices due to increasing production throughout the world. Industries using electronics range from those making computers to those making toys. The demand for quality ranges from zero failure for aerospace and certain computer applications to no requirement for some low-cost consumer devices.

Electronics vendors are spread throughout the world, so negotiating options available to buyers are extensive. Long-range contracts that are not tied to vendor cost and changes in technology may create serious problems for buyers. Finding and keeping high-quality reliable vendors may also be difficult during the last two decades of the twentieth century.

Quality is often the major negotiating issue for components. The failure rate of many components cannot be determined in advance; quite often the cause of failure is unknown. It may take a great deal of time to select a vendor with a reputation for maintaining quality and then reach an agreement on what is good quality.

Pricing of electronic components is often based on a buyer's total usage of a certain class of components rather than of just one component.

Where *precious metal (gold, silver, etc.) adders* are involved, fluctuations in the metal markets around the world may change the final selling price of electronic components. Buyers should determine the amount of precious metals actually used in a component and then negotiate a base market price for the precious metal. Since the selling price will vary as the market changes, the negotiations should establish how the market price will be determined—whether by date of component manufacture or by date of actual shipment. The price should be allowed to increase by only the actual extra cost, not the fully absorbed cost (see Chapter 2).

Buyers may prefer *functional performance* of electronic subassemblies as a standard, rather than component specification. This will put the burden for assuring good performance on the vendor and allow the buyer to test for function. *Liability for future failure* is an important consideration for many buyers. For certain critical applications this liability may be negotiated.

Restrictions on a distributor's sources may be required to ensure that standardized components are supplied. Many distributors obtain components from all over the world and have wide variations in quality. Buyers must determine how wide a quality variation they can accept.

Repair and inspection reimbursement to the buyer from the seller may be a negotiable issue, particularly for the import of electronics from certain parts of the world.

Replacement of rejected products (watches, calculators) is often cheaper than repair. Buyers should negotiate vendor's obligations with regard to rejections and replacement.

Special packaging of components may be required to accommodate the automatic insertion of components into subassemblies (circuit boards) or final assemblies.

Research and development projects authorizing the vendor to develop new technology and to produce an unknown product can be based on cost negotiation, with future pricing based on improvement curve analyses for a certain predetermined rate of experience.

Contract Assembly and Packaging Negotiations

Many companies purchase the manufacturing capacity for assembling and packaging products. This type of contract is an alternative to the investment of capital in new manufacturing facilities or improvements to older facilities. Vendors range in size and sophistication from sheltered workshops for the retarded to large, specialty food and chemical packaging companies that may be the principal packagers for all users of a particular product. The major negotiation issue is often what percentage of the vendor's total capacity will be allocated to the buyer's requirements.

Raw materials may be supplied by either the buyer or the seller. If the seller supplies the raw materials, the buyer should negotiate the percentage that the seller will add to the material cost. *Raw material security* may be a problem, particularly if the vendor is producing the same product for many customers or is using a common component such as an aerosol gas. Many buyers negotiate for a weekly or monthly inventory status report. Buyers also should seek the right to audit their inventory at the vendor's warehouse to verify the stock status.

Production losses of the buyer's inventory may occur through rejected production or through inventory "shrinkage." The vendor's liability for lost inventory must be agreed on before the contract is signed. The vendor may be responsible for all losses above a certain level and also for costs of all materials that have to be discarded because of defective production.

Buyer-vendor cooperation in *production scheduling,* including hooking the vendor into the buyer's computerized production control system, is fairly common. Buyers must have the right to schedule their portions of the vendor's production, within reason.

Sanitary requirements and liability for product recalls and consumer harm must be defined for all food processing. The vendor may be required to obtain a Food and Drug Administration permit and to submit to federal and state health inspections.

Access to the vendor's facilities for inspection, verification of performance, or inventory auditing is usually very important.

Product distribution to the buyer's customers or satellite locations is often handled by the contract vendor. The buyer may want the vendor to list the buyer's company as the shipper and use the buyer's documentation for the shipping papers.

The selling price is normally determined by marking up labor and machine utilization. Cost negotiations are very effective for this type of purchase.

MAINTENANCE, REPAIR, AND OPERATIONAL SUPPLIES (MRO)

MRO supplies usually account for the largest number of purchase orders but cost less than purchases in any of the other categories.

They comprise the major purchases of service businesses such as banks, insurance companies, or schools.

Vendors who sell MRO are usually industrial distributors, manufacturers who make spare parts for machinery and equipment, service divisions of original equipment manufacturers, and commercial printers. Because the vendors are often asked to deliver with little or no advance notification, they generally put more emphasis on service than on price. In most industries, the majority of MRO purchases are from industrial distributors.

Many innovative distributors are offering buyers simplified systems for ordering supplies. These systems ensure long-term business for the distributor and provide the buyer's company with a method of buying low-cost items without cumbersome paperwork procedures. The term *systems contracts* is used to define many of these simplified systems. Many distributors also have systems with other names such as data-phone, etc.

Normally, the most efficient way of buying is through the negotiation of annual contracts, which simplify repetitive purchases of items such as office or maintenance supplies, pipe or fuel. This is particularly true for materials from industrial distributors. There are very few places in North America that have only one industrial distributor for a specific category of supplies. Distributors generally sell from a standard catalog of items. Acceptable substitutes can usually be found if a vendor is out of stock of a certain item. Pricing variations among distributors are often small.

Many times buyers feel that price competition justifies having many suppliers. We have seen quite a few cases where buyers spend more money getting competitive bids during the course of a year than they save by having multiple sources. Finding new sources is usually relatively simple. If a buyer were to give all his or her business to one supplier based on competitive quotations and negotiations, he or she probably could change sources very quickly if the selected source failed to perform.

The buyer should support annual supply contracts for supplies whenever possible. Vendors should be selected by competitive quotations based on estimated annual usage by dollars and/or items. These annual contracts should be negotiated in order to establish a close business relationship and reduce the total cost of buying supplies.

Systems Contracts

The objective of systems contracts is to reduce the unit cost of the items being purchased and the overall cost of purchasing the items by a simplified releasing and paperwork procedure. The details of these contracts cover most of the repetitive problems buyers are confronted with—ranging from vendor service levels to emergency coverage to paperwork processing procedures. Some of the benefits of systems contracts include:

1. Reduced inventory,
2. Reduced costs of materials,
3. Reduced cost to buy,
4. Reduced paperwork,
5. Increased payment time,
6. Elimination of repetitive problems,
7. Advance planning for resolution of emergencies,
8. Increased user involvement.

Negotiation Issues for Systems Contracts

There are a number of negotiation issues for systems contracts. The *specific items* and *range of items* that the vendor will supply must be resolved. A buyer may want a vendor to stock a specific inventory of an item that is used only by the buyer's company. The vendor may ask the buyer to guarantee this special inventory; the negotiations should resolve the extent of the guarantee and the quantity or the percentage of the total forecasted usage to be stocked. Vendors may attempt to add to the contract certain related categories of items that the buyer uses but would like to buy elsewhere.

Vendor inventory levels must be sufficient for the buyer's requirements. The range and volume of inventory are critical to contract success. The buyer should resolve the degree of commitment to accept the inventory, particularly if items are used by many of the vendor's customers. The vendor should be responsible for reporting changes in inventory levels that affect the buyer's service levels. Buyers often negotiate the right to inspect the vendor's inventory in order to verify that it is adequate. What is adequate must be defined in the contract.

The *right to substitute* equivalent items of the same or higher value may be an issue raised by the vendor. The buyer may agree to the substitution as long as the price does not increase and the buyer has the right to approve all substitutions before the shipment is made by the vendor. *Purchases of similar materials not included in the contract* may also be necessary before the contract expires. The issue of how these items will be handled and priced by the vendor should be covered.

The *delivery service* issues include the percentage of items and percentage of each item that will be shipped within the negotiated lead time. Performance criteria should be established and agreed on for measurement of delivery service.

Back orders are a major problem for many companies. The buyer may wish to negotiate so that the vendor does not ship back orders and that the buyer can consider each item complete after the vendor has shipped a partial shipment. This normally is handled by agreeing with the vendor that the partial shipment will be priced at the price level for the original quantity ordered and that the buyer will reorder the item when it is needed again. In these types of agreements vendor performance is often measured against a preestablished quantity service level over a period of time. If the buyer must have a complete shipment, he or she should negotiate how long the vendor has to complete back orders. If the vendor does not complete a specific back order within a specified time, the buyer should have the right to go to the vendor's competition without violating the contract.

An *emergency order procedure* to cover the handling of orders that must be shipped in less than the normal lead time is often required. Vendors may wish to restrict emergencies to a limited percentage of the total orders to prevent all orders from turning into emergencies. The buyer may wish to include a night or weekend provision in the procedure if the company has problems that can occur outside of normal business hours.

Pricing may be at the vendor's cost plus a percentage markup or at the vendor's list price less a fixed discount.

The vendor and buyer should agree on *price stability,* along with how price increases are to be implemented and approved. In a cost-plus contract, the buyer may require the right to audit the vendor's costs by seeing copies of the vendor's purchase orders or invoices. Cost-plus pricing may also be based on average costs over a period.

When one is dealing with large vendors, *specific vendor sales service contacts* may be helpful in ensuring that the buyer's company will receive the service desired.

Within the buyer's company, *identification of the authorized releasers* is required if the ordering function is delegated. This is common in many systems contracts. *Vendor's responsibility to audit releases* for dollar limit and proper authorization is also required when releasing is delegated. A list of authorized releasers should be in the contract. This ensures that nonauthorized personnel do not release materials. If releasing is delegated, controls have to be designed into the contract to ensure that the company's interests are not violated.

Special paperwork, including simplified release, shipping, and invoicing documents, is often used. The vendor must agree to use the special paperwork. The procedures for handling the special paperwork must be a part of the final contract.

Special reports of business activity by the requisitioner are very helpful to the buyer when he or she is evaluating contract performance. Many vendors will provide these reports monthly as part of the contract.

A *special catalog* may be required by the buyer to assist requisitioners in ordering and to facilitate invoice processing activities of accounts payable. Responsibility for production and maintenance of the catalog may be negotiated.

Renewal and cancellation conditions related to service, pricing, and so on are required. These conditions are, of course, based on all other negotiated issues, but they should be discussed separately.

SUMMARY

There are many issues that can be negotiated with vendors. The type of purchase, personality of the vendor, and category of purchase define what is to to be negotiated. Buyers should keep in mind that all activities in the buying-selling relationship, from specification design to currency of final payment, are negotiable. Buyers should select the issues very carefully and include the requisitioners' interests and inputs in order to make sure that all business problems are covered.

Following is a listing of major negotiable items by category of purchase.

ALL NEGOTIATIONS

Price—pricing customs, increases

Volume

Transportation

Selling terms

Letters of credit

Services, delivery

Warehousing

Scheduling/vendor capacity

Quality
Replacement of defective materials
Warranties
Contract enforcement/cancellation

CONSTRUCTION AND CONTRACTUAL SERVICES

Profit through markup of labor, subcontractors on purchased materials and equipment
Performance criteria
Changes and additions
Fixed price/cost plus fixed profit
Type of labor
Warranty
Access to property
Contractor's work facilities
Insurance
Progress reporting
Extent of contractor's services
Escalation costs
Licenses and permits
Working hours
Overtime payments
Installed equipment title transfer and patent infringements
Facility and equipment start-up
Cleanup after completion
Force majeure
Liens
What is included and excluded from contract
Incentives and penalties
Delay changes
Labor costs and productivity
Markup percentages
Buyer's rights to audit contractor
Scope of services
Spare parts
Routine, preventive maintenance

Emergency maintenance
Extent of warranty work
Buyer's rights to work on equipment
Loaner equipment

CAPITAL MACHINERY AND EQUIPMENT

Performance
Installation
Start-up
Training
Specifications for electric, air, or gas
Blueprints
Government regulation conformance
Prepayment and final payment schedules
Spare parts availability
Local purchase of spare parts
Vendor maintenance
Warranty
Title to transfer point
Freight and insurance charges
Import duties and licenses
Delivery date
Cancellation liabilities
Price

INVENTORY FOR RESALE: ALL TYPES OF INVENTORY

Cost reduction or stabilization
Reduction of buyer's inventory investment
Delivery quantities
Extended payment terms
Assurance of supply
Quality
Overruns and underruns

INVENTORY FOR RESALE: PRICE LIST INDUSTRIES

Special packaging
Timing of vendor production
Right to spot-buy
Long-term contracts
Total pricing
Changes in specifications
Allocations during shortages
Consignment
Warehousing
Material-handling equipment

INVENTORY FOR RESALE: FABRICATED WOOD, METAL, AND PLASTICS

Raw material specifications and cost
Buyer-supplied raw materials
Tooling quality, size, and cost
Tooling ownership and maintenance
Quality standards
Vendor's production methods
Vendor's capacity allocation
Warehousing of raw materials and work in process by vendor
Liability for cancellation

INVENTORY FOR RESALE: PRINTING

Formula pricing
Specifications
Color control and variations
Warehousing
Preparatory costs
Paper supply and cost
Automatic assembly machinery performance
Document security

Performance and regulatory compliance
Right to inspect
Drop shipments
National contract agreements

INVENTORY FOR RESALE: ELECTRONIC COMPONENTS AND SUBASSEMBLIES

Quality
Pricing
Precious metal adders
Functional performance
Distributor's original sources
Future liability
Repair and inspection reimbursement
Replacement of rejects
Special packaging
Research and development

INVENTORY FOR RESALE: CONTRACT ASSEMBLY AND PACKAGING

Vendor's capacity allocation
Raw material supply
Raw material security
Production losses
Production scheduling
Sanitary requirements
Product recall liability
Product distribution
Cost/price factors
Buyer's access to vendor's facility

MAINTENANCE, REPAIR, AND OPERATING SUPPLIES (MRO)

Annual supply
Special inventory
Usage guarantee

Right to substitute items
New items not in existing contract
Delivery service
Back orders
Emergency orders
Pricing
Price stability
Sales service support
Special paperwork and report procedures
Vendor responsibilities to audit releases
Catalogs
Renewal
Cancellation

The above items are intended to form the basis of a buyer's considerations before entering into negotiations. Almost every negotiation will have additional items that are specific to the buyer's company. A measurement of a buyer's creative skill is his or her identification and inclusion of those items.

4

Planning for Negotiation

The essence of any successful endeavor is planning. Power, in purchasing, comes from two sources—dollar volume and knowledge. The planning process is probably the most important dimension of negotiation because, when properly done, it forces the acquisition of knowledge. Through proper planning the buyer can negate the inherent knowledge advantages traditionally held by the sellers.

The buyer must always keep in mind that the seller normally comes into a negotiation with an advantage in industry knowledge over the buyer. The seller has the advantages of dealing in a single industry and having access to detailed cost and profit information. The buyer, on the other hand, is usually forced to be proficient in several industries.

Detailed planning is the equalizer. Without it, the buyer will never be able to compete with the seller on equal terms. The planning process offers the buyer the opportunity to develop goals well in advance of the actual negotiation, to develop a strategy, and to decide on the tactical approach to be taken during the negotiation.

In order for planning to be successful, adequate time must be allocated. If it appears that there will not be sufficient time to do a proper planning job, the buyer should do everything possible to avoid going into a negotiation. If there is sufficient time to postpone the purchase, do it. If the time frame is such that there must be some interim coverage, attempt to make a spot purchase to gain preparation time.

It is essential that the buyer go into a negotiation with a well-defined list of objectives. Although it may sound simple on the surface, the process of selecting objectives can be complicated because there are so many external factors. There is no "school solution" to the setting of objectives. Objectives involve the buyer's needs, the company's demands, the company's profit picture, the buyer's relationship with the supplier and amount of interest in preserving this relationship, the competitive conditions in the industry, domestic and worldwide economic conditions, and the buyer's level of knowledge about the industry. It is therefore essential that the buyer develop definite objectives prior to a negotiation.

Although the development of objectives is only one part of the planning process, it is vital. Since no two people think, plan, or react alike, we have tried to develop a system of negotiation planning that can be used by anyone at any level of complexity. The buyer can use all of the planning system or just part of it and go into a negotiation prepared.

The planning system consists of four major parts or steps. These four steps are designed to provide a mental checklist which the buyer can review each time there is an imminent negotiation. Depending on the complexity of the negotiation, all four steps may not be used. However, each step should be at least mentally reviewed before a decision is made to eliminate that particular part of the preparation process. The system is simple to remember, easy to work with.

The four basic steps for negotiation planning follow this sequence:

1. Set objectives.
2. Analyze the positions expected from the other side.
3. Select and use a team (optional).
4. Finalize planning by evaluating the objectives established in steps 1 and 2, and collecting more background data on them.

In the following pages each of these basic steps will be explored and guidelines offered so the buyer can maximize the contribution of each step to the planning process.

STEP ONE—SETTING OBJECTIVES

The process of setting objectives will vary in complexity depending on the industry, the dollar volume of the contract, the technical requirements, the economic condition of the buyer's company, the directives from purchasing management, the situation in the seller's industry, and the general economic conditions. Add to all of these factors the needs of the buyer in terms of fulfillment of personal goals, desires for achievement, and interest in preserving or not preserving the relationship with the seller, and the true complexity of setting objectives becomes apparent.

The first step for the buyer is to make a realistic appraisal of the situation. The buyer should analyze his or her needs on a professional level.

The buyer should then try to gain a perspective on the overall situation. In this phase the buyer and his or her associates should spend some time brainstorming the possibilities of the upcoming negotiation based on an analysis of where they are and where they want to go. This brainstorming technique can be a useful device for the buyer because it provides input from people who may be intimately involved in or quite knowledgeable about a given industry. However, even the inquiry of an industry outsider who is seeking to understand some point may provide the buyer with an insight, an approach, or even the recognition of a potential hazard. The ability of the buyer to communicate, to ask questions, to involve others in the situation can be most valuable.

At the same time, the buyer should be actively researching. The well-organized purchasing department should operate as an in-house intelligence agency: collecting, collating, evaluating, and, when expedient, disseminating information. To be a successful negotiator, the buyer must work hard to acquire all of the industry data possible. Knowledge is power! The end purpose of this period of brainstorming, information collection, and evaluation is to permit the buyer to develop a realistic perspective on the power situation in the forthcoming negotiation. The buyer can thus discover any weaknesses in the buyer's and seller's positions and gather more information if a weakness is on the buying side of the fence. A buyer's failure to accurately appraise the buying position can result in some unpleasant surprises at negotiation time.

Possible Objectives

In developing objectives, the buyer will discover that objectives fall into such categories, as base pricing, logistical demands, quality and performance control, transportation details, technical demands, and warranties and disclaimers. Following are some suggestions for objectives in these areas.

Pricing

The *base price* for items is a key pricing objective and one of the major issues in negotiation. Other pricing objectives include discounts, rebate agreements, payment terms, billing arrangements, escalator and de-escalator clauses, and price limiting clauses.

Every industry has its own way of pricing and doing business. The *discount schedule* for volume purchasing is usually related to the number of items purchased. *Rebate agreements or schedules* relate to the dollar volume of the agreement. This is another form of the discount schedule. If this approach is used, the buyer must be sure that the agreement is spelled out in detail so that there is no misunderstanding.

Payment terms are becoming a more important area for negotiation. The cost of money, particularly in short-term borrowing, is having a radical impact on the cash flow of many companies. The ability to negotiate an extension of terms can have the effect of an extra discount on the purchase.

Delayed billing, where the product is produced and shipped at a given time but not billed until a later date, is often a viable negotiation objective. Delayed billing usually occurs in seasonal industries where advance running of supplies such as packaging materials is necessary. Usually the concession of delayed billing is tied to a provision that allows the seller to produce the items or materials during a slack time or at the convenience of the seller.

Escalator/de-escalator clauses for raw material and labor cost adjustments are becoming more common. It is difficult now to get a seller to agree to a fixed price for a given period or to a fixed percentage price adjustment schedule for a fixed period. As a result, the escalator clause is gaining popularity. The key to the escalator, particularly for raw materials, is that it be indexed either to a privately published industry index or to a government published index for the particular raw material.

For raw materials, the escalator/de-escalator formula should be tied to the percentage of the total cost represented by the raw material cost. Rarely does raw material cost constitute 100 percent of the cost of the product. The buyer must determine the percentage of the total cost credited to raw material and develop a formula incorporating that figure, with increases in raw material prices tied to some index. For example, suppose raw material cost comprises 70 percent of the cost of the product. The allowable price increase should be 70 percent of the percent increase in cost of the raw material. Thus if the raw material published index price rises 10 percent, the allowable increase under the 70 percent approach would be 70 percent of the 10 percent increase, or 7 percent. This is a fair and workable approach that accurately reflects the impact of the raw material cost increase on the product cost.

Escalator clauses for labor are more difficult to negotiate. The buyer is really at a disadvantage here because it is difficult to ascertain the true effect of the labor cost increase on the end price of the product. The safest approach is to use the Department of Labor rate scales for the industry. This information is readily available at a local federal government information center. The rate scales for the industry and the geographic area can be applied in formula to the product cost structure. The buyer should find out what percentage labor costs are of the total manufacturing cost. Once this is known, the buyer has a fighting chance to develop some kind of approach to the problem.

Restrictive clauses to limit price increases are becoming increasingly important targets for negotiation. Consider the following approaches to limiting price increases. Bear in mind that these are not the only types of restrictive clauses; they are simply designed to provoke thought on the development of clauses for particular industries.

1. To limit price increases, use a clause that puts a limit, usually a percentage figure, on the right of the seller to raise prices. This clause should prevent the increases from exceeding the named percentage.

2. A clause may be used to limit the seller's right to raise prices on shipments made or scheduled to be made after *x* date.

3. If the buyer wants to retain the right to approve all price increases, the clause should read roughly as follows: "The seller's right to increase the price is controlled since all price increases must be approved by the buyer prior to the shipment of any orders." As a protective device, the buyer should include some language covering the situation where the buyer and the seller cannot agree on a new price, in which case the buyer should have the right to cancel the balance of the order without being in breach of the contract.

4. Escalation clauses can be tied to indexes published privately or by the government. If this is desired, the buyer should indicate in the clause that, if during the length of the contract there should be increases in labor costs or materials, as indicated by either private indexes from trade periodicals or indexes from the Department of Labor or the Commerce Department, then price escalation action can be initiated.

5. Clauses can be used to force suppliers to justify requests for increased prices. This increasingly popular approach has been adopted as modus operandi by many purchasing departments in the last few years. The advantage of this restriction is that it often gives the buyer insight into the cost structures of the seller. Such a clause might contain language something like this: "Suppliers requesting increases in selling prices must provide information to the buyer indicating where the price increase is occurring, i.e., materials, labor, fuel, variable costs, fixed costs, indirect labor, overhead, or whatever class of costs is impacting on the pricing." This information is of value for future negotiations and an aid in the development of more accurate cost estimates for verification of seller claims on costs and pricing. This also eventually creates a psychological barrier in the mind of the seller and tends to limit the presentation of any frivolous requests for price adjustments. Sellers will be very reluctant to divulge actual cost information. A demand for cost justification generally places the seller in a defensive position.

Never hesitate to negotiate on any aspect of cost or pricing deemed of economic value. However, a basic understanding of costs in the industry is essential if such attempts to negotiate cost items are to be successful.

Logistical Needs

Supply need objectives involve delivery schedules, lead times, make and hold arrangements, consignment shipments, special arrangements, expansion agreements, and cancellation clauses.

Delivery schedules are vital. It has become increasingly popular in industrial purchasing to negotiate penalty clauses for the shipper's failure to deliver on time. This practice has long been part of construction contracts. The apparent lack of appreciation by industrial sellers of the importance of holding to specified delivery dates (a common buyer complaint) has made penalty clause negotiation almost a necessity. Even if the clause cannot be negotiated—and it is difficult—at least the buyer can signal concern over the need for on-time delivery. *The establishment of lead times for materials* is a viable negotiating issue related to the ultimate delivery date. It can be a workable vehicle for the buyer in negotiating a firm delivery date.

Make and hold arrangements for finished goods are negotiable. With money as expensive as it is today, holding the finished goods may be tied into a schedule of payments during the holding period. Although it may be difficult for the buyer to negotiate a make and hold arrangement completely at the seller's expense, the attempt should be made.

Consignment shipments are a relatively new arrangement in industrial purchasing. Consignment has long been a way of life in the resale industries. Usually the consignment concept can be applied to a product if it has two basic characteristics:

1. The usage is constant year in and year out.

2. The lead times on the product are quite long. In these cases, the buyer stocks the inventory on the buyer's premises and pays for the material as it is used. This is merely a variation on the make and hold theme, but the buyer may have to do some selling to convince the vendor. It is customary to offer some sort of concession to the seller in terms of either a long-term contract, an allowance of automatic replacement shipments on a prearranged schedule, or partial payment at a specified percentage when each shipment is received. This alternative is very beneficial for the buyer and should be explored whenever possible.

Special arrangements for stocking and distribution of products fall under this category. These arrangements, which can be valuable to a buyer, are often tied to the stocking arrangements of the seller. The buyer can negotiate on such concepts as:

1. Seller ships to seller's distribution points and allows buyer's plants to draw from these points.

2. Seller arranges to drop ship to buyer's plants or distribution points instead of bulk shipping to the buyer and forcing the buyer to handle the distribution.

Any special arrangements suited to a particular industry or the usage pattern of the buyer can also be negotiated.

Clauses to allow for expansion of volume are also subjects for negotiation. Normally there will be some concomitant arrangements for price negotiation with an *expansion clause.*

Cancellation clauses should be clearly delineated, with specifics about time allowances for notice of cancellation by either party, and how and where the notification is to be given. When ordering equipment with a long lead time one is wise to negotiate a cancellation settlement in advance. Sometimes such equipment, because of the lead time, is ordered in advance of the approval of the capital investment budget. This is generally done by a letter of intent. A cancellation schedule can be negotiated at the same time. Since there is always the possibility that the item may not survive the budget review, it is best to be prepared for this contingency.

Quality and Quality Control

Quality objectives revolve around such points as specifications, rejection notifications, liability, and inspection techniques.

Specifications and allowable variations are often at the heart of agreements about machinery and equipment. They are also usually the hardest issues to negotiate. When setting quality objectives the buyer is wise to seek a great deal of input from the engineering unit. For instance, *performance specifications* provide a fertile ground for controversy unless they are specifically negotiated into the agreement. If equipment has to perform at a given level, such performance must be clearly spelled out in the agreement. If it is not, even though there may have been either verbal or written representations that such performance capability was within the range of the equipment, the question of whether or not there was an express warranty could well lead to litigation. A specific agreement eliminates this possibility.

Test specifications and criteria for rejection of products should also be negotiated. Whenever there is the possibility for rejection of materials based on preliminary testing, the buyer and seller must agree on the test procedures and what data results will constitute grounds for rejection. The method of notification of rejection and seller's required action are also legitimate objectives for negotiation. Rejections are prime subjects for lawsuits; anticipatory action can save much expense and management time.

Liability clauses for faulty material or equipment are becoming items of intense negotiation these days. Some recent court decisions regarding product liability have had far-reaching effects. Arguments over rejections usually revolve around whether the defects are substantial enough to warrant rejection, whether the seller was given a chance to "cure" the defects, whether the buyer specified the defects to the seller, whether the buyer notified the seller promptly, and whether the buyer protected the goods until the seller could remove them from the buyer's premises. The respective positions of both parties in the event of subsequent liability for faulty material or equipment should be spelled out. The normal negotiating approach is for the buyer to attempt to negotiate a "hold harmless" clause to come into effect in the event of subsequent litigation resulting from damage or injury to a third party due to an equipment or material failure.

Agreement on inspection techniques is also negotiable. If there is a desired inspection technique, it should be negotiated and made part of the agreement.

Transportation

Transportation should be purchased just like any other commodity. Depending on the industry, delivery arrangements can have a significant impact on the total cost of an item. Thus the terms of sale specified by the buyer can have long-range effects on the transaction. Transportation details include FOB point, classification of freight, and packaging considerations.

The FOB point is very important in terms of when possession takes place, when title is transferred, who pays the freight, and who follows up on claims in the event of damage by the carrier. Buyers should be aware of the common terms and their implications. The following chart indicates the impact of the various transportation terms of sale.

Terms	Where Title Passes	Who Pays Freight
FOB buyer's plant Freight collect Freight allowed	Buyer's plant	Seller initially Eventually buyer
FOB buyer's plant Freight collect	Buyer's plant	Buyer
FOB buyer's plant Freight prepaid	Buyer's plant	Seller
FOB seller's plant Freight prepaid	Seller's plant	Seller
FOB seller's plant Freight prepaid and charged back	Buyer's plant	Buyer
FOB seller's plant Freight collect	Seller's plant	Buyer

Transportation terms are items for negotiation. Often the buyer will want to equalize freight costs between various locations, with the objective of maintaining a standard price at all locations. The buyer may sometimes want the right to designate the carrier as well.

Determination of the freight classification can be a subject for negotiation. The freight classification, especially when the potential freight costs are high, can have a heavy economic impact. Control of this cost aspect can significantly affect the overall cost structure of the agreement.

Clauses covering *packaging* are also important. In negotiating packaging, consider such questions as what preparatory costs will be assumed by the buyer and what by the seller, delivery schedules, makeready charges, costs for proofs, film costs, plate costs, cylinder costs if the job is roto-gravure, ownership of the films and plates or cylinders, allowable overruns. In addition, both parties should make clear what kind of lighting specifications are to be used in viewing both proofs and the final product. If both parties are not using identical light sources, it will be impossible to match the proofs to the final production. It is suggested that agreement be made to use the International Standard of 5000 kelvins, which is what is used in the vast majority of printing plants. Differing light sources can compound the problem of proofing, and reproofing is an expensive process.

Technical Demands

Technical support demands in the agreement may range from inconsequential ones to those essential for success, depending on the type of business, the in-house capability of the buyer's company, and the capabilities of the seller to render technological support.

Research and development support, depending on its importance to the buyer's company, can be a fundamental objective. Negotiation may revolve around type of support, seller's charges, reporting systems, and length of support (for one project or many). Negotiations should determine who pays the bill if the seller must go to outside experts. The possibilities are almost endless.

Engineering support is often a matter for negotiation, particularly where the buyer must depend heavily on the supplier's engineers for input about an item or piece of equipment. The buyer must be aware of all of the engineering costs that could accrue, such as those for drafting time, use of outside experts, the making of models and mock-ups, sample tooling, purchase of drawings, and samples. The buyer should consider who owns the rights to the systems, processes, or ideas created while the buyer's company is working with a supplier's engineers. If necessary, there should be some agreement as to the ownership of patents for items or processes developed in the course of the project.

We recommend that the buyer take full advantage of the advice of legal counsel, particularly if questions of proprietary rights, ownership of tools, models, designs, and the like are concerned.

This is a very complicated area where the buyer may well run afoul of established industry practices concerning ownership of production components. The buyer must attempt to negotiate ownership of all components whenever possible, regardless of industry practice. It is recommended that the buyer adopt a basic negotiating stance of "If I am paying for it, I own it." Although this will lead to controversy in many cases, the buyer must be prepared to stand and fight.

It is axiomatic that the buyer must control as many of the costs as possible. Tools, dies, designs, films, plates, mock-ups, models, roto-gravure cylinders, special jigs, and drawings that are charged to the job and paid for by the buyer are costs and must be controlled. Failure to secure ownership of production tools will deprive the buyer of flexibility in the marketplace and place the buyer in a single source situation. The buyer's company must have the option to move tools if necessary to protect the company's economic well-being.

Warranties and Disclaimers

Warranties and disclaimers of warranty are fast becoming critical areas of dispute. Since there are ever-increasing attempts by suppliers to negate the effects of warranties, the buyer should remain constantly aware of the basics of warranty.

There are three kinds of warranty used today under the Uniform Commercial Code. They apply in every state except Louisiana. (Louisiana has not accepted the Code and still operates under the common law concepts of warranty.) Under the Code, there are three types of warranty.

The express warranty is created when a seller makes a written or verbal representation as to quality, specifications, or performance specifications which influences the buyer to purchase the product. Typical examples:

"These tires are good for 40,000 miles before they need to be replaced."

"This machine will produce 3,000 of part *x* per hour."

"All parts of this machine that will come in contact with food are stainless steel."

The express warranty can be created by advertising pieces, sales representations, or responses to requests for bid where detailed specifications are given.

The implied warranty of merchantability prevails on every product. It is a blanket warranty for the buyer that entitles the buyer to expect "fair quality" goods. While "fair quality" does not sound particularly encouraging, it is better than no warranty at all.

The implied warranty of merchantability for a specific purpose is created when a seller develops and sells a product to perform a particular function.

Warranty disclaimers come in a variety of packages and attempt to limit the liability of the seller. The buyer must watch out for these disclaimers. Upon seeing a disclaimer, the buyer must take immediate steps to counteract it or else suffer a severe limitation on the warranty protection. Warranties are covered in detail in Chapter 6.

The setting of objectives is a complicated process which should be given as much time as possible and considered judgment. How well the objectives are developed will set the pattern for the negotiation. The settlement ranges on objectives should be sufficiently wide to allow room for movement during the negotiation. Ill-defined or vague objectives will lead to an unsatisfactory negotiation and will almost always result in the buyer's failing to do the best possible job for the company.

STEP TWO—ANALYZING THE POSITIONS EXPECTED FROM THE OTHER SIDE

The buyer's approach to position analysis will undoubtedly depend on the buyer's experience level, his or her ability to evaluate the myriad of factors involved, the industry involved, the industry's economic situation, and the overall buyer-seller relationship.

This area of preparation generally causes the most difficulty for the buyer, as it requires a great deal of work and the gathering of industry intelligence. However, it is vital for the success of the negotiation that this phase be completed. The information derived will affect objectives, the makeup of the team (if used), the collection of further information, and, ultimately, the conduct of the negotiation.

Basically, the buyer must try to determine the wants and the needs of the seller. These wants and needs will suggest what objectives the seller will probably have, the potential areas where concessions might be gained, areas where negotiation should succeed, and the expectation levels of the seller.

To adequately attack this problem, the buyer must make both an industry analysis and a seller analysis. Following our step-by-step approach will give the buyer the bulk of the information needed to be prepared for the seller's probable points. Since the last thing a buyer needs in a negotiation is to be surprised, the old saying of "forewarned is forearmed" should be heeded.

The Industry Analysis

An industry analysis allows the buyer to discover conditions in the industry and then evaluate the seller's position relative to the industry. There are almost endless possibilities for collecting and evaluating information, but for simplicity's sake only key checkpoints will be discussed. If time permits and if the buyer desires, individualized checkpoints can be added to best serve the particular needs of the buyer.

The Overall Condition of the Industry

To find out about the overall condition of the industry, the buyer should investigate sales and growth patterns and raw material sources. What is the *sales pattern* of the industry? Is the economic picture strong? Are sales and backlogs holding up? What is the outlook for next year and possibly the year after?

The buyer should also attempt to find information about the potential *growth pattern* in the industry. In these days of extensive governmental interference in business, potential restrictions, such as EPA restrictions, can have a long-range effect on the growth potential of an industry. Look at the new construction planned or in process. Is there potential for increased production in the near future? If there is, it could indicate a possibility of increased competition in the industry and potential bargaining points for the buyer. On the other hand, if a declining capacity situation is developing, the buyer might change basic objectives in the face of a possible shortage.

The *raw material situation* of a given industry should be of vital interest to the buyer. Buying today is a worldwide operation. So many of the raw materials come from offshore that the buyer must make an effort to be aware of the availability of supplies at all times. If a key industry receives much of its materials from offshore sources, the buyer's approach to negotiating for service of supply is different from that used if the raw material is readily available locally. Enlightened self-interest dictates the necessity for intimate supply information as a keystone for planning.

The Industry's Relation to the National Economic Situation

The condition of the national economy and predictions about it for at least the next year are essential information. Certain industries are hit harder in a recession than others. Knowing how an industry reacts under economic pressure is very important to the buyer, since the whole pattern of setting key objectives can be influenced by this. Industry reaction to an economic downturn will affect the buyer's expectation level, the type of planning to be done, and the general level of aggression in the negotiation.

Conversely, if the economy is strong, the seller's position will most likely be firmer and the approach more positive, with concession possibilities restricted or reduced. Thus, general economic conditions weigh heavily in the planning process.

Supplier Analysis

The second analysis is of the supplier. There are some basic points that should be checked about the supplier prior to a negotiation.

Review the performance history of the seller for the past year. Normally a purchasing department will have some system for evaluating seller performance. It may be extremely sophisticated, with complete computer records on deliveries, pricing, competitive stature, and quality performance, or it may be a relatively casual objective-subjective appraisal of overall performance level. There is an increasing tendency to temper the strictly mechanical appraisal with some subjective comments based on evaluations of the quality of administrative assistance offered (reports, inventories, and the like) and the vendor's reactions to problems and crisis situations over the year. Often the strictly mechanical evaluation fails to fully define the relationship's more subtle aspects.

Research the supplier—from attitudes to business cycles. In this evaluation, the buyer must analyze the attitudes of the key supplier personnel and try to perceive the overall philosophy of the company. Some companies tend to be aggressive and well managed, leading their field with the newest in technology and responding to the needs of the buyer. Other companies, while well-managed and profitable, seem to always function as followers, not leaders. While this may not affect whether or not the buyer wishes to use the supplier, it will affect how the buyer conducts the negotiations.

A supplier analysis is not something the buyer does once a year. It should be an ongoing activity, reviewed once a year as part of the planning process. The buyer should make every attempt to visit the supplier's facilities as often as possible throughout the year. These visits offer the buyer a golden opportunity to develop a composite picture of the true attitude of the supplier. The buyer should make a point of talking at length with personnel other than those in the sales department. Here the buyer will be able to discover just how the supplier looks at the buyer's account. The more important the account is to the supplier, the better the bargaining position of the buyer will be. The supplier's attitude about and ranking of the buyer's account can have a tremendous effect on the buyer's ability to negotiate.

On any visit to a supplier, the alert buyer will always keep in mind the need to gather information. No piece of information is so minor that it shouldn't be tucked away for future reference. Intelligence estimates are not made up of large chunks of information that clearly lay out the situation. Instead, they are painstakingly constructed from bits and pieces of seemingly extraneous information until a perspective on the situation finally develops. Be ever curious and ask questions so that a pattern develops; eventually the supplier will give more information in anticipation of questions. Once a supplier begins to see a buyer as someone with constant intellectual curiosity, he or she will give information more easily.

The buyer should always start with basic questions. Find out the *general business forecast* for the company. Always have a copy of the annual report on file. Learn to read and understand the data in the annual report; it contains a gold mine of information. The financial people in the buyer's company should teach purchasing personnel the basics of financial analysis.

Check the supplier's plans for expansion or withdrawal from the market. Check the timetable of increased production capability for forewarnings of increased competition in the industry in the future.

Check production cycle trends. Is there a time (or times) during the year when the supplier's business is traditionally slow? Is there a cyclical fluctuation that occurs on a regular basis from year to year? This type of information should suggest the proper times for negotiations. Never schedule a negotiation during the peak of the supplier's production cycle. Always select a time when the supplier's machine operators are washing windows or repainting the lines on the factory floor. If there is a predictable production cycle with clearly defined high and low periods, the buyer may be able to indulge in contra-cyclical buying. This is a valuable negotiating tool because it offers flexibility to the buyer and the supplier. In essence, the buyer offers the supplier the chance to make products during the low cycle or at his or her convenience. In return, the buyer can negotiate a fistful of advantages. For example, the buyer could negotiate for supplier storage, reduced costs, supplier-managed distribution, delayed billing, or freight equalization. The prospects are limited only by the knowledge, imagination, and aggressiveness of the buyer!

There should be no limitation on the efforts of the buyer to collect, catalog, and evaluate information. After all, the supplier is doing precisely the same thing. For years, suppliers have been teaching their people that knowledge of the buyer's company, products, operating philosophies, and future plans is essential for superior salespeople. The suppliers always try to be well informed about the buyer's company and industry. Knowing this, can a buyer afford to be less informed and ill-prepared at negotiation time?

Developing the Supplier's Objectives

The goal of the information-gathering and evaluation process is the discovery of the supplier's probable objectives. Once the buyer has a feel for the supplier's industry, the national economic picture, the availability of raw materials, the economic conditions in the industry, and the outlook for the near term, he or she can determine probable objectives of the supplier.

The buyer should determine objectives for the supplier in the same way the buyer set his or her own objectives. However, there is one complication. The buyer's objectives must now be weighed against the objectives of the supplier. The buyer may have to make some adjustments in his or her own objectives after analyzing the other side's. There is nothing wrong with this. Remember, the idea is to find attainable objectives that will maximize the economic benefits to the company. There is no room for pig-headed obstinacy or inflexibility. Try to be as realistic as possible when determining the supplier's objectives. It may be a revealing experience; most certainly it will point out areas in the buyer's plans that need revision or rethinking.

STEP THREE—USING A TEAM (OPTIONAL)

The use of a team in negotiations is not a new concept. It has been a way of life in labor negotiation for many years and is becoming more popular in industrial negotiation. It is true that most of the negotiations which an average buyer will conduct will be of the one-on-one variety, but there may be times when a team approach will be the most beneficial method. Therefore, it is best to be prepared to use a team when needed. The following guidelines give basics for use of a team. Team negotiations are effective from two standpoints. First, there is the psychological advantage of having more bodies at the table. Second, there is the practical advantage of being able to use special talents that various team members bring to the team.

Guidelines for Team Selection

Team selection should be based on the expected complexity of the negotiations and the need for expert advice from professional disciplines outside of the purchasing ranks. Team members can be selected from almost any area of the company, such as engineering, production, cost control, production planning, marketing, accounting, sales, new product development, quality control, material management, or management consultants.

In selecting the team, the buyer should consider the following factors:

1. The complexity of the item(s) being purchased.
2. The purchasing objectives.
3. The supplier's potential positions and objectives.
4. The economic impact of the purchase on the company.
5. The possible areas where concessions may have to be granted or can be obtained. If the concession areas are highly technical in nature, involving specifications and possible changes in specifications, there should be technical advice available on the team.
6. Knowledge of the negotiating habits of the supplier. If the supplier normally brings several people to the table, the buyer should have an equal body count to balance the situation.
7. The buyer's own evaluation of the need for expert advice to support the negotiation.
8. The buyer's comfort level with the use of the team. If the buyer is not really comfortable or confident using a team, yet the situation indicates a need for technical support, the buyer should keep the team to a minimum, regardless of what the supplier does in terms of team personnel.

Utilizing the Team Approach

The use of the team enables the buyer, who is always the team leader, to do a variety of things in preparation for the actual negotiation:

- Use the input from the various skills represented in refining purchasing objectives.
- Distribute tasks in the information-gathering phase. Team members should research the objectives closest to their respective disciplines.
- Use the team members to brainstorm the potential supplier positions and objectives.

After information gathering and objective setting have been completed, the team leader should "role play" the negotiation. In a complicated negotiation, advance role playing can help eliminate surprises at the actual negotiation. The devil's advocate technique is the approach normally used in role playing.

The team leader should also evaluate how well the team members have prepared for the negotiation. He or she should determine whether there are any weak links in the team—members who may not be able to present arguments and ideas adequately during the actual negotiation.

In actual negotiation, the use of the team gives the buyer several advantages. By dividing up responsibility for the presentations of various objectives among the team members, the buyer divests the other team of the opportunity to concentrate on one person. This dilutes the application of power by the supplier team. It is difficult to concentrate pressure when there are several areas requiring pressure. If the buyer is alone, he or she has little chance to quietly observe, listen, and evaluate the opposing positions. When on a team, the buyer has more time to think and observe and thus is more likely to catch possible mistakes by the other team, slight position changes, and supplier reactions to the various points advocated by the buying team. To control the team and orchestrate the negotiation, the buyer must have time to listen and concentrate.

Naturally there are some disadvantages to using the team. The first problem is the selection of the team. The buyer must bear the full responsibility for selecting, preparing, briefing, coaching, and controlling the team. There is always the possibility that some team member will speak at the wrong time, inadvertently revealing information. Not all of the team members may be comfortable as advocates; this will result in a less confident front being presented. Add to this the buyer's problem of monitoring the research activities of the team and it is evident that the buyer has his or her hands full making a team function as a well-drilled unit.

The buyer must weigh advantages and disadvantages in deciding when to use the team method. If the team technique is chosen, team capabilities should be used to the fullest. Team negotiations are a powerful weapon in the buyer's arsenal.

STEP FOUR—FINALIZING PLANNING

The two operations involved in the last step—finalizing planning—are evaluating objectives and collecting more information.

Evaluating Objectives

Objectives fall into several categories depending on economic importance and viability. Most important, of course, is the economic impact of the objective. The need to obtain a given objective is directly related to the economic gain or loss tied to that particular objective. Objectives fall into three major classifications.

Primary objectives are those objectives that are essential to the economic well-being of the company and that must be realized if the negotiation is to be a success.

Secondary objectives, as a class, are important and will have an economic impact. However, there is generally more room to negotiate with this type of objective. In actual practice, the bulk of the give and take in the negotiation will be on secondary objectives.

Tradeables are selected with two major purposes in mind. First, the tradeable gives the buyer something he or she can trade away without suffering economic damage—a tradeable should be exchanged for a concession on an objective of higher rank. Second, a tradeable may be inserted in a negotiation disguised as a more important objective for the purpose of forcing a discussion on a point which may be of a confrontational nature. For example, if the buyer desires to remove a contract point which has been in effect and which is of benefit to the seller, a seller reaction can be expected. If the seller is reluctant to discuss the point, the introduction of a tradeable, usually of an unacceptable nature, will often force a discussion of the original point. Once the desired concession has been gained on the original point, the tradeable may be conceded or withdrawn from the negotiation. Tradeables are valuable tools if properly used.

The buyer must first *classify and rank all his or her own objectives*. Each objective should be placed in its proper category, depending on its economic impact.

The supplier's objectives should then be classified in the same manner, using the latest information available. The same ranking procedure should be performed. It is essential that the buyer determine the ranking of the supplier's objectives, as this will affect the last phase of preparation: researching information to support the buyer's objectives.

Once the objectives have been ranked, it is now time to *take each objective and develop a negotiating position on it*. It is essential that the buyer be aware of his or her relative position on any given objective at any given time. The usual approach is to take each objective and set a maximum, middle, and minimum position. The middle position usually represents the point of settlement hoped for in the original objective-setting procedure.

The position ranges are affected by many factors, including the cost needs of the buyer, the marketplace situation, the situation in the buyer's company, and the overall negotiating objective for the buyer's company. For the sake of illustration, assume that a buyer realizes that a price increase is inevitable. The early evaluation phase indicates that 6 percent seems to be the probable final level, so it is this level the buyer wants to obtain by the end of the negotiations. The buyer might therefore set 6 percent for the middle level, perhaps 8 percent as a maximum level, and 0 percent as the desired minimum level.

The buyer should also *set maximum, middle, and minimum positions for the probable objectives of the supplier,* and chart them in relation to the buyer's expectations. The charting process allows the buyer to quickly identify any areas where his or her expectation levels are too far from the expected supplier settlement zones indicated on the chart. Such a major disparity in settlement ranges has within it the seeds of a deadlock, which both sides want to avoid. If this situation occurs, the buyer may have to rethink and reevaluate the desired settlement ranges in terms of the expected positions of the seller. Assuming the buyer was reasonably accurate in anticipating supplier demands, the buyer should now be able to estimate how far apart the parties are on given objectives, what will be truly difficult to negotiate, and what the buyer's true expectation levels should be. The closer together the ranges are, the better the chance for agreement is.

The next step for the buyer, after ranking, charting, and evaluating the supplier's objectives, is to take a realistic look at each objective and calculate the realistic potential of concession before settling on a final level of concession. In the process, the buyer should estimate how far the supplier can be tested before he or she will take a final stance. This final evaluation is a valuable planning device—it gives the buyer a chance to check over the settlement ranges and make any necessary adjustments before he or she embarks on the final information-gathering phase of the planning process.

Collecting More Information

Information collection is one of the most important parts of preparation for negotiation. It is here that the buyer can gain control even before the negotiation starts. The better prepared the buyer is, the easier the negotiations will be. Since the bulk of negotiation revolves around some aspect of cost, it is absolutely essential that the buyer have a complete grasp of what constitutes manufacturing cost. Remember, since almost any aspect of manufacturing cost is negotiable, the buyer must understand the basics of costing. Cost items must be clearly defined, especially in a complicated negotiation. The buyer should review manufacturing costs in order to seek out potential areas or points of cost for negotiation.

Familiarity with manufacturing costs also gives the buyer a headstart in assembling cost data for the future. Knowledge of costs in a given industry or for a given supplier is of utmost importance to the buyer, because this knowledge gives the buyer control at negotiations. However, cost information is generally regarded as the preserve of the supplier, to be jealously guarded and protected. Thus this is the one area where an adversary relationship may develop between the buyer and the seller.

SUMMARY

Planning is the key to successful negotiation. Without proper and adequate planning, the buyer will invariably end up giving away the store. The ground rules are simple:

Set objectives. To set objectives, brainstorm with colleagues and analyze conditions pertaining to the negotiation. Research your own company's needs and goals as well as those for the industry involved. Objectives generally fall into the categories of pricing, supply needs, quality control, shipping details, technical demands, and warranties and disclaimers.

Analyze the positions expected from the other side. Try to determine, as accurately as possible, the objectives of the seller. This is best accomplished through detailed industry and supplier analyses.

Use a team, if feasible. The use of a team gives the buyer the practical advantage of adding special skills to the buyer's side and the psychological advantage of having more personnel to confront the seller.

Evaluate objectives and collect more information. Objectives come in three ranks, primary, secondary, and tertiary, or "tradeables." All objectives should be ranked, and for each objective at least three levels of potential settlement should be established—maximum, middle, and minimum. This enables the buyer to have a constant feel for where the negotiation is going. The complexity of the final information gathering is dictated by the activities and needs developed in the preceding steps. Above all—be thorough. It is better to have more information than necessary than to have too little.

Planning is a learning device for the buyer. There is always room to increase knowledge; never be caught short in that department.

5

Personalities
and Negotiation

A negotiation is a contest governed by no specific rules. Power levels affect gains and concessions, but in theory each side should be a winner. The current win-win philosophy is based on a premise that if a relationship between a buyer and a seller is to endure, each party must walk away from the negotiating table reasonably satisfied. This approach contrasts directly with some of the former attitudes toward the buyer-seller relationship. Buyers and sellers assumed that they had to be antagonists and that it was up to each to gain as much as possible—even if it was to the extreme detriment of the other! Times have changed; purchasing departments have become more sophisticated and the selling side has gained in knowledge and talent. Buyers have realized the merit of developing long-term working relationships with good suppliers. (Suppliers have sought this for years and have always included it as part of their planning.) As buyers have learned more about the financial aspects of business, they have realized that it is not good business practice to deprive a supplier of a reasonable profit.

Although the win-win theory is now the basis for most negotiation, one party can win a little more than the other. In every transaction between people, simple or complicated, it is normal for one party to emerge with more than the other. How much more depends on a variety of factors. Some of the factors that affect negotiation are tangible, such as dollar volume, length of contract, the buyer's knowledge of the industry and product, and the relative impact of the purchase on the overall business of the supplier. There are also intangible factors in every negotiation, which can and do affect the final outcome. These intangibles are the psychological aspects of negotiation, such as negotiator's estimate of self-worth, confidence levels, perception and comprehen-

91

sion of power, understanding of the various types of personalities, evaluation of individuals' needs, and understanding of the characteristics of a good negotiator.

A sound negotiation starts with the negotiator. It is essential that the buyer have a true picture of his or her strengths and weaknesses and self-esteem before entering negotiation. However, self-analysis is an exercise that should be performed whether negotiations are involved or not. It is necessary for planning a career, improving one's current situation, evaluating one's performance, and determining what training must be acquired to counter weaknesses and meet the demands of the marketplace for the future. It is difficult to face up to weaknesses and possibly damage one's ego in the process. No one likes to acknowledge that there are some aspects of his or her makeup that are found wanting. No one likes to face the cold facts of failure in any area. Nonetheless, the buyer must evaluate his or her traits in relation to the key traits of superior performers and try to see where he or she needs improvement.

Honest and aggressive self-evaluation is the first step toward reaching one's potential. It should be followed by a programmed and disciplined approach to improvement for areas requiring attitudinal change. The key motivational factor must be the realization and the acceptance of the fact that each of us can be whatever he or she wants to be, if we are willing to make the sacrifices necessary. Performance is a matter of attitude. The motivation for performance must start with the individual. Although systems, philosophies, techniques, formulas and the like have been written on how to motivate people, they fail to recognize a basic fact of life—the only one who can truly motivate an individual is that person alone. However, efforts by others to "motivate" someone may provide the catalyst to start the individual in considering the need for improvement, which in turn may lead to the person actively working on the problem. The following guideline for self-evaluation is a basic list to which each person can add other attitudes or attributes deemed important.

SELF-EVALUATION ATTITUDINAL GUIDELINE

Self-Esteem

Self-esteem is the foundation of high-performance behavior. Do you see yourself as valuable, worthy, capable? Do you feel that you can accomplish just about anything you really set out to do? Do you feel that you deserve success because the decisions you make and the actions you take are solid and in keeping with your own and the company's objectives? Do you actively seek challenge, or are you passive, reacting only when presented with a challenge? Do you feel that you can change or control the conditions that lead to your success?

Responsibility

How responsible are you? Do you initiate events that account for your successes or failures? Do you acknowledge your accountability, both when things go right and when they seem to fall apart despite your best efforts? Can you analyze the reasons for your successes or your errors?

Optimism

Optimism is related to general confidence level. Do you feel that things will be better tomorrow? Do you feel that you guide your destiny to a great extent, and, as a result, the future will be bright, productive and profitable? Do you invest your time and talent to the fullest? Do you believe that today's investment will most assuredly bring tomorrow's rewards?

Goal Orientation

Many people set goals but never reach them. The superior performer handles goals differently from other people. The secret of the high achiever is that he or she places the goals in a system for accomplishment so that the goals are always visible and achievable. Do you use goals as motivational devices? Do you behave according to a pattern designed for meeting your goals?

Awareness

Being goal oriented, do you absorb information from what is happening around you? Are you aware of the clues and road signs that constantly surround you? Are you aware of the opportunities for reaching your goals? Do you make good use of all of the clues, signals, and opportunities that abound in business, the community, your home life, and leisure time?

Creativeness

Are you creative when searching for solutions to problems? Are you creative in finding the best ways of getting along with people? Handling people calls for a level of creative introspection that is difficult to develop. Do you continually search for new approaches and new opportunities, even when faced with the opposition of those who are always against change in any form?

Communication Ability

Are you a good communicator? Do you take the time to think your ideas through, then explain them clearly? Are you a good listener? Do you make the effort to clear your mind of extraneous thoughts and concentrate on what the other person is really saying? Do you have empathy for the other person?

Growth Orientation

Have you accepted the fact that it is impossible to stand still and be successful? Those who resist change remain in place. These are the traditional defenders of the status quo, the ones who refuse to grow because there is risk in growing. What are your priorities? Do you give high priority to the job of getting ready for the future? Do you welcome the chance to trade old unproductive ways of doing things for new techniques and thought patterns?

Response to Pressure

How do you respond to pressure? When the deadlines close in, when there is a need for a decision or action to solve a problem, how do you react? Do you rise to the occasion, actually welcoming the pressure? Some people perform better under pressure; they seem to relish the excitement. Do you perform smoothly under pressure, or is it a time of crisis for you? When you are under pressure, do you feel stressed beyond your comfort or confidence level? Do you have to actively "handle" stress or do you accommodate stress as a normal part of life?

Trust

Do you really trust people? Do you sincerely feel that people don't, as a rule, try to do badly? Do you feel an atmosphere of trust in most aspects of your life? Are you comfortable in giving responsibility to another member of the team and trusting that person to perform well? Do you cooperate in your relationships with others?

Risk Taking

Do you accept and live by the principle that life has no guarantees? Are you ready to reach out and take reasonable risks? Are you prepared to live with the success or failure of a decision? Have you mastered the art of weighing alternatives prior to making a final decision? Are you reasonably confident as to your ability to make sound decisions?

This is an initial self-evaluation checklist. We have not attempted to list every question that should be asked. Our objective is to provide some stimulating questions in each of the categories.

SELF-EVALUATION AND ASPIRATION LEVELS

Why be concerned about self-evaluation as a part of negotiations? Self-evaluation helps an individual recognize strengths and set goals, and aspiration levels are directly related to the individual's confidence and ability to set goals. Experience has proven that the buyer who enters a negotiation with a high expectation level will generally emerge with a larger share of the pie than one who has no such aspirations.

People with solid self-images will never enter a negotiation with the idea of coming out second best. The goals they set are high. To do less would be a betrayal of their self-images, and result in loss of self-respect.

People set goals not only for negotiation, but for almost every aspect of life. There are business goals—in terms of status, income, rank, privileges, and the like. There are also social goals, which generally reflect the attainment of business goals. Social goals are evidenced by type of housing, cars, club memberships, status in the "social register," and similar indicators. Although the choice of aspirations is a personal one, the individual is usually influenced by work environment, business associates, the person's past-performance record, and the performance record of the peer group in which the person functions. These factors are reference points for determining and measuring the aspirations of a given individual.

As noted previously, aspiration levels are a factor in the ultimate success or failure of a negotiation. Changes in an individual's aspiration level will correlate with the level of success or failure attained in a given situation. Most people determine their aspiration levels by attempting to balance the need for accomplishment and the desire for rewards against risk and the possibility of failure.

It is in this weighing process that self-image becomes an important factor. The strength of the individual's feelings of worth will determine how much the individual will influence the chances of success. Goal-oriented people tend to set goals that permit them to exercise their full range of skills; they feel that the outcome of any activity will be the result of their ability to control as many aspects of the situation as possible. They do not fear failure as do those with lesser self-images. Those who lack confidence tend to dwell on the negative aspects of a situation. Therefore, they tend to set less ambitious goals so the risk of failure and its consequences can be reduced. If goals are low, one cannot fail as an individual, but one does fail in the larger sense—one fails to exploit opportunities to the fullest on behalf of one's company.

To summarize, a good self-image derived through honest self-analysis is one of the cornerstones of a successful negotiator. The perception of worth builds confidence and permits the individual to set goals that are in line with this higher aspiration level. The successful negotiator will be able to evaluate which risks should be taken. He or she will have the need to achieve—the hallmark of the superior performer. This person will be able to persist in the pursuit of goals. Recognizing the impact of his or her own self-image and need for achievement on negotiations, the negotiator can begin to work on these traits of the opponent, with every action and concession geared to reducing the expectation level of the other side.

PERSONALITY EVALUATION AND NEED RECOGNITION

Since negotiation depends largely on people on the other side of the table, the buyer must be able to recognize and catalog the basic personality types of the opposition. This enables the buyer to adjust attitudes and approaches as the negotiation proceeds. The determination of the other side's need levels, on an individual basis, can be quite useful to the buyer.

The ability of the buyer to understand the opponent is based on the buyer's discovery of the attitudes, opinions, emotions, and temperament of both the opponent and the buyer. Part of self-analysis is ferreting out and recognizing one's own attitudes, opinions, emotions, and general temperament. Until this is done, the buyer will have difficulty in discovering the needs of the sellers, let alone developing a clear picture of the personalities involved.

The buyer must use every communication skill available to assist in the analysis of the personalities of the sellers. The most important communication skill involved is the art of listening. Although much has been said about the need to be a good listener, it is a relatively undeveloped skill with most people. Listening is very hard work and is a learned skill rather than an inherited one. Remember, you do not learn anything when you are talking. Listening is not only a communication device that permits the buyer to acquire information, but also a good negotiating technique.

Besides being a good listener, the buyer should become a solid communicator. This does not imply that the buyer must be a silver-tongued orator, but it does mean that the buyer owes it to the company to make sure that every time he or she communicates, the meaning and intent are clear. A well-thought-out strategy of buyer counteraction, based on personality evaluation and need assessment, depends for its impact on effective communication.

How the buyer approaches the problem of performing and using a personality evaluation and need assessment depends on the individual mental processes of the buyer. However, there are some logical checkpoints that should enter into the process. For the sake of organizational clarity, the process can be approached in the following manner:

1. Assess attitudes, opinions, emotions, and temperament. Usually one's initial opinion is formed on the basis of one's reaction to factors in these four categories.

2. Recognize the personality type of the seller.

3. Gauge the seller's probable needs based on conclusions from the previous steps.

4. Use the evaluations on personality and need to plan the process of the negotiation. Develop a system to utilize the personality and probable needs of the supplier to bolster the buyer-seller relationship.

ATTITUDES, OPINIONS, EMOTIONS, AND TEMPERAMENT

Attitudes may be defined as a set pattern of actions or thoughts which tend to be emotional in nature. Attitudes are generally learned, not inherited. The important thing for the buyer to remember in dealing with attitudes is that they usually do not respond to logical thought. People develop attitudes toward other people, religious or political situations, life conditions, or concepts without the application of logic and reasoning. Attitudes are composed of opinions, prejudices, and beliefs developed and nurtured by experience and environment.

One major problem in dealing with attitudes is that the person may not even realize that he or she has a particular attitude. Very often attitudes result in active dislikes and fears about people, economic positions, religions, politics, ethnic backgrounds, and other characteristics.

Attitudes form the basis of most of the prejudices that people have. It is advisable to walk carefully in the presence of attitudes, and it is generally useless to attempt to change them. The buyer should always be aware of the explosive potential involved in attempting to combat an attitude of another person. If attitudes are introduced into the negotiation, their deep emotional content can be disruptive.

Opinions are much easier to deal with than attitudes. In general, opinions are developed through the process of thought and reasoning. Granted, the thought may not always contain the best of logic, but at least there is an element of reason which is lacking in attitudes.

People are generally aware of their opinions and, in most cases, are open to a reasonable and logical discussion of them. Opinions can be changed by logic and reason; attitudes usually cannot. The ability to differentiate between attitudes and opinions is an important negotiating device for the buyer.

Emotions are the inner feelings or disturbances that lead to definite reactions, generally of a physical nature. Recognition of an emotional response in a seller is important to a buyer. The buyer should study the seller's "body language" in order to gauge emotional response to a given statement or situation. Emotions affect people more than attitudes or opinions, since they are the most noticeable expressions. People tend to react emotionally in a characteristic manner—for example, an individual may become very quiet when angry.

The ability to determine another's emotional response to a given stimulus is of great importance to the buyer: The buyer who understands the emotional makeup of an opponent has a negotiating weapon of great value. The ability to play on the emotions of another and to predict the other's response is an advantage that cannot be underestimated. There are times in a negotiation when the buyer may want to inject some emotionalism for a tactical purpose; knowing what will trigger such a response is a definite tactical advantage. People who become emotional in a negotiation universally wind up on the losing end. There is no room in negotiations for temper or emotion of such intensity that the person loses the ability to reason logically.

Temperament is a completely different problem. Often irascible people are referred to as temperamental. However, this is not correct—they are really "emotional."

Temperament generally is viewed as the peculiarly individual physical and mental organization of a person, which permanently affects the person's thinking, feeling, and acting. Temperament is the natural disposition of a person unaffected by extraneous pressures. The easiest way for the buyer to determine another's temperament is to note the personality traits that appear to comprise the attitudinal approach of the person. The buyer's recognition of distinct personality signals will lead to the development of a personality profile for the individual.

PERSONALITY TYPES

The individual's personality type is directly related to his or her need level; the buyer must therefore be able to quickly categorize each one of his or her opponents, at least superficially, at the outset. Identification in depth will occur as the relationship lengthens. The buyer should look for identifying strengths and weaknesses from each personality type. These are the keys to determining needs for the immediate situation. Each party, the buyer included, will have a series of needs which he or she would like fulfilled, in whole or in part. If the buyer can partially meet the needs of the seller, even though the seller is unaware of these needs, the buyer may gain concessions favorable to the company. It is very difficult for the average person to correctly identify these needs without first performing the intense self-analysis mentioned earlier.

Although it is impossible to place each person in a comfortable niche with clearly defined personality traits, there are general category types that seem to cover most people. There will always be some characteristics that evade neat classification. The following is intended to be a general guide to readily identifiable personality types. It is designed to provide a quick identification system for initial evaluation of a given individual.

THE POWER SEEKERS

The power seekers are usually easily recognized by their unrelenting drive to achieve results. Power seekers tend to be very insensitive to the needs, feelings, and reactions of other people. These people are definitely high achievers, with little empathy toward people who do not exhibit the same drive and ambition. Normally this type of person is very difficult to deal with in negotiations, since he or she will give little room for the recognition of another's position. Power seekers are generally singleminded in their approach to what they consider to be the proper solution to a given problem. They tend to be impatient with others who want to develop another approach or position. Power seekers are basically self-centered and dominant. They are willing to exert power in order to achieve desired ends and may even be ruthless in the pursuit of predetermined goals. The buyer will probably find negotiation with this type of person to be very trying.

When the buyer realizes that there is a possible confrontation brewing with a power seeker, he or she must develop a strategy for counteracting the expected power assault. In planning such a strategy, the buyer must pinpoint the wants and needs of the power seeker with care. Use the following guide to recognize the interests and probable stress areas of the power seeker.

Needs and Weaknesses

Power

Power is the dominant need. In most instances, power seekers will not compromise on who is to be the one in authority. Control of every situation is essential to them. Attempts to diminish control or dilute authority will be met with fierce opposition. This drive is so powerful that it can sometimes lead to a variety of problems, the most common of which is a bitter confrontation.

The Trappings of Power

External evidence of power and prestige is very important to power seekers. This may be in the form of the office and its furnishings, use of a company limousine (usually with chauffeur), membership in the most prestigious clubs, or expensive homes, clothing, jewelry, and the like. There will be an interesting mix of business and social manifestations of the need for prestige. An interest in money and material things is a classic feature of this type of personality.

Challenge

The need for constant challenges is another dominant factor in power seekers. Challenge is the sustenance from which power seekers draw vitality. Challenge offers power seekers the opportunity to demonstrate their capabilities and build their egos through the accomplishment of difficult tasks. The opportunity to confront and control a challenge provides the power seeker with the means to develop, expand, and hold power. The holding of power also provides the rationale for accepting the trappings of power and prestige. Therefore, power seekers not only need challenge but are dedicated to it as an essential for existence and future growth.

Power seekers always need difficult assignments—the tougher, the better. They also need to tackle the unknown. This type of person is the ideal sounding board for new ideas and concepts, particularly when there is a large element of risk. Power seekers seem to be fascinated by moving into uncharted ground, probably because of their need for challenge and their need to constantly demonstrate superior ability in getting results.

Use of Decision-Making Ability

Making decisions is no problem for power seekers. Decisions are recognized as a form of challenge and, as such, are handled with assurance and confidence. Power seekers have a definite advantage over most people because of this ability to make decisions. For many people, decision making is traumatic. They hesitate, procrastinate, resist change, and do anything to avoid making the decision. This predilection in others provides power seekers with the proper atmosphere. Power seekers move in, fill the decision void, get results, and in the end add to and consolidate their power base. On the other hand, if power seekers are placed in a situation where the opportunity to make key decisions is restricted or minimal, they will not stay long in the company. If the climate is not right, power seekers will move on.

Results

Power seekers are results-oriented. In a sense, they have a definite need to get results and to see a project completed. Power seekers will be impatient with delays. Bureaucratic approaches have no place with this type of person. The power seeker's compulsion is for action—to get the job done as quickly as possible and get on to the next major situation. This drive for constant action makes life very difficult for the people who have to work with power seekers.

It takes a very special kind of person to understand the pressures and needs of the power seeker. There must be a personal commitment to the power seeker or personality clashes will rupture any relationship.

Use of Problem-Solving Abilities

Problem-solving ability is one of the strengths of power seekers. Solving problems is equivalent to getting results, and it gives power seekers great satisfaction. Cost reductions would be high on the priority scale for this type of person. The chance to explore alternative ways of cutting costs is a challenge power seekers would consider worthy of their time and effort.

To summarize, power seekers are usually very dominant. Used to getting things done, they are results-oriented and impatient with those people or circumstances that thwart their efforts toward resolving a problem. These are venturesome people, unafraid of moving into the unknown. Challenge is the key to power seekers. Power seekers tend to run roughshod over less forceful types of personalities. They have little concern for the feelings or opinions of others.

This type of person will not usually weigh risks carefully. Because of their supreme confidence, power seekers tend to consider risks as annoyances to be ignored so that a problem can be resolved. Caution is a word that does not exist in power seekers' vocabulary. Power seekers also prefer not to delve too deeply into facts since such activity may delay results. Decisions are made quickly, firmly, and without undue deliberation.

This analysis of the needs and wants of power seekers is not intended to be unflattering. The intent is simply to deal with the fact that such dominant personalities tend to arouse hostile feelings in those who must deal with them. There is a definite place for this type of person in the business world. Power seekers are the doers who are brought in to revive a failing operation, to spearhead a risky new venture, or to rebuild a company that has fallen victim to apathy, status quo, and atrophy.

It will be a real challenge for the buyer to negotiate with this type of person. The ever present risk of an unpleasant confrontation makes negotiation a tension-filled experience. However, there are ways for the buyer to exploit the characteristics of a power seeker. It takes some careful analysis, planning, and preparation. A game plan should be designed to play on all of the foibles of the individual and to diminish the potential for excessive controversy.

Buyer Counteractions

Negotiation with a power seeker should be planned so that it exploits his or her talents and satisfies as many of the power seeker's needs as possible. Using his or her knowledge of the power seeker's needs, the buyer should be able to gain many concessions.

The basic approach to the negotiation is the key.

The buyer should bear in mind the power seeker's need for:

power and its trappings

challenge

use of decision-making abilities

results

use of problem-solving abilities

the excitement of the unknown (receptivity to new ideas)

Consider the potential weaknesses:

tendency not to weigh risks thoroughly

lack of caution

impatience with delays

tendency not to delve too deeply into the facts

tendency to dominate associates

need to be recognized as the leading character in the negotiation

tendency toward angry confrontation

General Strategy and Approach

The buyer's general strategy should be to involve both sides in a session more geared to problem solving than to negotiation. A fact-finding approach will usually be well received by the dominant person. The buyer should use these themes:

"We have a fine relationship which we all want to preserve. However, there are some problems that must be solved." (Appeal to the problem-solving proclivities.)

"We appreciate the fact that you [dominant character] are here to lend your talents and prestige to these proceedings. The problems are complicated and there is a need for sound decisions." (Appeal to needs for prestige, challenge, and decision making.)

"Buyer analysis of the problems indicates that this may be the time for consideration of some innovative changes in the way things are done." (Challenge with the unknown.)

The buyer should also consider using the following techniques to exploit the power seeker's weaknesses during the session.

Support points with as much documentation as possible, particularly complicated cost figures.

Be prepared to be very patient. Once there is a proposal on the table, stick to the position with tenacity.

If applicable, have an innovative proposal or two ready to throw out on the table. Try to get a discussion going on new approaches if it appears that things are bogging down or if tension is building toward a possible confrontation.

Do not provide much information regarding possible risks initially. Force the other side to develop potential risk positions.

If the other side is using a team, *concentrate on the team leader initially* to play on his or her need for prestige. As things progress and it gets closer to concession time, *concentrate on the team members and appear to bypass the leader.* This will cause the dominant personality to become uneasy about losing his or her place in the forefront, and he or she will try to regain the leadership. It is at this time that favorable concessions will be made. Often, in regaining the leadership, the power seeker will make concessions without too much thought of the consequences. To the dominant personality, the limelight and action are necessities. The buyer must take away the leadership at some time in the negotiation. Once the tactic works, the buyer should never be the one to restore leadership to the other team's leader. Force him or her to seize the reins.

When regaining the leadership role, the power seeker will create dissension in the other team and strengthen the buyer's position. Thus, patience in negotiating with dominant personalities is essential. Since the power seeker dislikes inaction, he or she will take steps to establish an action atmosphere—and this will involve making concessions in order to obtain measurable results. Playing on the weaknesses of the power seeker is the best tactic for the buyer. Attempts to deal in a direct way with issues will invariably lead to confrontation, which is not conducive to good negotiations. A shouting match does not lead to agreement but to stalemate and eventual disruption of the relationship.

If there is no team involved, the buyer might alter the approach and *try to keep the negotiation a problem-solving session.* The buyer should set the mood in the opening remarks by listing problem areas. Obviously all the items listed will not be serious trouble spots. However, they all will be tied in with the buyer's objectives.

It is important to remember, no matter what approach is used, that head-on confrontations should be avoided if at all possible. By appealing to the problem-solving interests of this type of person, the buyer can fulfill another's needs and achieve the predetermined objectives.

Finally, if a confrontation becomes inevitable, do not back away. The power seeker will usually attempt to run roughshod over the opposition. It is here that the ability of the buyer becomes important. The buyer should:

1. Listen. It serves no purpose to get into a raging debate. There can be no negotiation when one of the parties loses control. Therefore, the best counter is for the buyer to listen and take notes. This is an interesting maneuver, since it tends to cause some concern on the part of the speaker. Remember, much of the rhetoric the buyer will hear is for effect. It is designed to overpower. Note-taking has a defusing effect. Even if the speech is mainly for effect, the buyer should listen carefully. Sometimes, out of anger or frustration, the power seeker will drop an important piece of information. Listen also for *what is not said*. Often what is left out or ignored is just as important as what is said. Regardless, there is no substitute for intelligent listening.

2. Do not interrupt, even if statements are inflammatory, untrue, or outright lies. Keep cool and collected; do not become emotionally involved. The power seeker's objective is to upset the buyer, establish dominance at the negotiating table, and force concessions from the buyer. It is a tactic as old as time, and one which is usually successful. Most people dread a head-on confrontation. Those who know how to use confrontation and are at ease with it, such as the power seeker, will invariably end up dominating any buyer who cannot handle discord and dissent.

3. Be prepared to use the questioning technique whenever the power seeker stops his or her speech-making. This is the purpose of taking notes. It indicates that the supplier was listened to (courtesy), but that the buyer was unaffected (coolness). Questioning, particularly with the use of notes, has a most disquieting effect on the dominant individual. Thus the buyer can diffuse the tension and regain control of the negotiation. The power seeker can and must be handled in a negotiation. However, the buyer must identify this type before negotiation in order to be properly prepared. It is too late to discover at

the table that there is a dominating powerhouse sitting across the room. Then there is no time to prepare or to plan how to counteract the tactics that will be used.

THE PERSUADERS

Persuaders are more familiar figures in the world of negotiation because their characteristics seem to fit more of the salespeople whom the buyer meets daily. In many ways, this type of person offers more problems to the buyer than does the power seeker. The power seeker is easily recognized as a potential threat to peace and harmony. Persuaders, on the other hand, are not confrontation specialists. Yet underneath that suave exterior generally lies a very ambitious person who will work very hard to fulfill needs.

It is generally more difficult to identify needs and weaknesses in these people. Their approach is subtle, low key, and designed to provide a settled atmosphere for negotiation. It takes a great deal more analysis by the buyer to identify needs, wants, and weaknesses. The need levels are usually buried under an exterior that exudes warmth and charm. Use the following guideline to identify the inner workings and needs of this type of individual.

Needs and Weaknesses

Personal Popularity

Personal popularity is a major need in persuaders. Such people have a deep-seated need to be liked. Some form of social recognition is very important. This type of person will go to almost any length to look good in the eyes of others.

Recognition of Ability Through Monetary Rewards

The trappings of power are important to these people for a reason different from that of power seekers. Power seekers need the accoutrements of power to assist in maintaining dominance or the appearance of continuing power, while persuaders need them as a form of reassurance. Personal popularity is so important to this type of person that any reduction in the external signs of continuing popularity will cause considerable apprehension. Monetary rewards are important because they provide persuaders with the means to acquire and maintain the visible symbols of popularity and accomplishment.

Constant Public Recognition of Ability

Persuaders need some form of constant reassurance that their abilities are being recognized and appreciated. They are always concerned about whether they have created a favorable impression. These people need some ego stroking to maintain morale and continue to perform at an outstanding level. This should not be construed as a weakness. We all like recognition of our abilities. However, with this type of person, the need seems to be somewhat stronger.

Interaction with People

Persuaders revel in interaction. They have a genuine desire to help people. They are interested in the techniques required to establish high motivation in people. This type of person is comfortable only in the constant company of people, in contrast to the power seeker, who regards people as necessary evils useful only as tools to get the job done.

Persuaders generally create a favorable working atmosphere for colleagues and subordinates. Their usual managerial style is some variation of "participative management." As a result, those who work with a persuader will be extremely loyal. Confidence and trust are evident in this type of person's relationships with subordinates and peers.

Freedom from Details

Persuaders are not usually detail-oriented and are uncomfortable in situations involving a great amount of detail. Their orientation is toward planning and the overall picture; persuaders prefer to leave the operational details to those better equipped to take care of them. Details are viewed as irritants that interfere with other activities of greater interest.

In summary, the persuader can be a formidable negotiating opponent. Buyers tend to be lulled into passivity because this type of person is easily liked. The trademarks of the persuader are articulateness, poise at all times, and general enthusiasm about the company, the product, and the people with whom he or she is dealing. It will be very difficult for the buyer to become antagonistic with persuaders, because such people generally present a persistent atmosphere of affability. This is the warm, charming, "good old boy," seemingly more interested in maintaining a good relationship with the buyer than in protecting the well-being of the company. However, this facade is most misleading, because under that cloak of favorable impression there generally lies an aggressive person keen on goal accomplishment. Persuaders have a strong commitment to obtaining the objectives they set for a negotiation, because reaching preset goals is evidence of ability. Ability is recognized in the business world—and the need for recognition is high with this person.

Buyer Counteractions

Negotiation with the persuader will generally be pleasant, tension-free, and productive. However, do not be lulled into a false sense of security by the agreeable atmosphere. Persuaders are dedicated to accomplishing their objectives and maximizing the results.

In the planning and analysis stages, the buyer should keep in mind the major need levels of this type of person:

personal popularity

recognition of ability through monetary rewards

constant public recognition of ability

interaction with people

freedom from details

Also consider the potential weaknesses:

dislike of working alone

disinterest in details, or research for detailed facts

difficulties with concentrating on the job at hand for prolonged periods

discomfort in an atmosphere of confrontation

tendency to withdraw in the face of aggressive or blunt behavior

General Strategy and Approach

In planning the approach to a negotiation with a persuader, try to reach a balance between fulfilling his or her needs and exploiting weaknesses.

Try to make this a one-on-one negotiation, if possible. A favorable power balance for the buyer can be created by playing on the seller's dislike of working alone. Anytime the opponent can be placed in a position of unease, there is an initial power advantage for the buyer.

Be prepared with a mass of details. When negotiating each point, ask for detailed information from the supplier. This will put more pressure on the persuader, who dislikes detail intensely. Often, by initiating a detailed approach, the buyer will gain concessions quickly because the persuader wants to see some evidence of progress.

Be prepared to use a certain amount of flattery, particularly when you are making a concession. Emphasize that you are reluctant to concede but are doing so because of the skill levels of the opposition. This ego stroking is a technique that works well with this type of personality. Persuaders need to have their ability recognized, and a little catering to this need will reap great rewards in the long run.

Be aggressive and blunt without being impolite. A businesslike approach from the beginning, with social amenities limited, will tend to put the supplier on the defensive. Gaining the upper hand without being obvious gives the buyer tremendous impetus in the negotiation. The no-nonsense, "let's get right at it" approach is disconcerting to the persuader.

Have patience. A lengthy negotiation is not to the liking of this type of person. The persuader prefers to handle things on a friendly basis. By denying this kind of atmosphere and sticking to a moderately brusque, businesslike conduct, the buyer will keep control of the negotiation.

When the seller seems to be hesitant about making a concession, *the buyer should not be afraid to initiate a semi-hostile attitude* in order to force the decision. It usually is not necessary to venture into a confrontation with people like this, because the threat is enough to get action.

THE RELIABLE PERFORMER

The reliable performer is a familiar figure in most companies. The buyer should keep in mind that not all negotiations involve external sources. The purchasing department, because of its working relationships throughout the organization, is constantly negotiating within the company. Negotiating within the company is often as important as outside negotiating. The buyer may meet the reliable performer often within the company.

It is rare for a buyer to encounter this steady personality as the leader of a negotiating team. However, there will almost certainly be at least one member of the team who will have the basic characteristics of this personality type. To identify the reliable performer, the buyer should look for the characteristics below.

Needs and Weaknesses

Maintenance of Status Quo

The reliable performer can be difficult to persuade of the value of any idea that seems to threaten the status quo. This kind of person usually accepts change with great reluctance, because change threatens the current situation.

Security in the Job

Maintaining job security is a need related to the desire to preserve the status quo. Reliable performers will view with distrust and downright alarm anything that seems to be a threat to their jobs. These people respond to confrontation by withdrawal, fear, and alarm. Confrontation threatens their security and leads to a defensive attitude.

Reliance on Historical Procedures

Reliable performers are content to do things the way they have always been done. If these people obtain a position of power, they can be serious deterrents to progress.

Constant Appreciation and Recognition

The need for recognition is basic to all of us, but it is greater with reliable performers. This is probably because this type of person fears any change that might be a threat to job security. The buyer should use constant approbation to build this type of person's confidence and provide reassurance.

Time to Adjust to Change

Since reliable performers need time to adjust to change, the buyer must carefully think out the negotiating approach in order to avoid the opposition's withdrawal in the face of new ideas or approaches. How ideas are presented to this type of personality is the key; slow and easy is the answer. Large quantities of patience are needed.

Organized Presentation

Reliable performers will respond to organized, detailed presentations that answer as many questions as possible. General concepts, theories, and far-ranging ideas will be rejected out of hand. Reliable performers are usually unable to think on a large scale. They prefer to focus on a narrow range of ideas, dissect them, digest them, and then take time for an adequate consideration before accepting them. An in-depth approach to a problem or a concept would be accepted, but a superficial presentation would not even be considered. The superficial approach leaves too many questions unanswered.

Limited Area of Responsibility

Reliable performers cannot control a large area of responsibility. They lack the conceptual ability to take progressive action in a large theater of operation. However, in a relatively confined operational area, this type of person works well. The reliable performer is almost the classic case of the perfect number two or three person. This kind of person can be very valuable to a leader with the wide-ranging conceptual approach. The reliable performer is a valuable stabilizer.

Reliable performers can be valuable contributors to the progress of a company, if properly controlled. They must not be allowed to consistently "man the barricades" against new and progressive ideas. These are people who need constant reassurance that all is well. Recognition of efforts is all important to them. Any idea, proposal, or concept presented must be well defined, detailed, and organized in the classic format of proposal, reasons, and conclusion. Anything less will be viewed as a threat to security and will be fought.

Do not be misled into thinking that this type of person is a pushover in a combative situation. They tend to be very resolute when they feel threatened and can be quite resourceful in coming up with defensive actions. The reliable performer's tendency, when threatened, is to react with near desperation to defend the status quo. This kind of person needs to work within long-established frameworks.

Buyer Counteractions

There are two keys to negotiating with the reliable performer—preparation and patience. The ability to keep one's temper is paramount. The buyer will most likely be frustrated because of the necessity of really "selling" an idea to this kind of person. The buyer's approach must be cautious, noncombative, and well organized. Keep in mind the needs and weaknesses.

The needs of the reliable performer include:

maintenance of status quo

security in the job

reliance on historical procedures
constant appreciation and recognition
time to adjust to change
organized presentation
limited area of responsibility

The weaknesses of the reliable performer include:

poor reactions to confrontation
limited ability to grasp wide-ranging concepts
reluctance to make decisions rapidly
reluctance to negotiate alone, need for support from able associates

General Strategy and Approach

In planning strategy and tactics for negotiations with a reliable performer, the buyer must really examine the person and try to identify as many needs and weaknesses as possible. This will be a tough negotiation in terms of emotional impact on the buyer. It is easy to get frustrated when dealing with reliable performers, but the buyer must be as patient as possible. For greatest success in negotiation with this type of personality, consider the following hints.

Try to have the negotiation on a one-on-one basis. This will remove the support factor so needed by the reliable performer.

Break the negotiation into small, well-defined objectives which can be handled with relative dispatch. Attempt to utilize every shortcut possible to arrive at an agreement. The longer the negotiation is, the more defensive the opposition will become. Thus, speed in reaching an agreement is the key to success. Avoid any attempt to negotiate wide-ranging objectives.

Be prepared with detailed data for bolstering the buying position. Present concise figures and foresee objections so you can answer them in advance.

Push for agreement constantly. This is disconcerting to reliable performers. Normally, speedy decisions are not their strong point. Care must be taken that the push not be too aggressive—too much pressure may cause the reliable performer to withdraw, and thus result in no agreement at all.

Depending on the buyer's analysis of the opposition, *confrontation can sometimes be very effective.* If the buyer feels that the seller will not completely withdraw, it makes sense to use pressure. *The most effective approach is to keep switching tactics.* Go from reason and conciliation to aggression and back again. The reliable performer does not adjust well to rapid situational changes.

However, if the buyer concludes that the aggressive approach would be a mistake, then *gentle persuasion is in order.* Be patient and understanding. Use some ego stroking, push gently for resolution, and give praise when an agreement is reached on a point. Use the needs of the reliable performer as planning and tactical operational tools. When dealing with this type of personality, the buyer is often better advised to fulfill needs than to exploit weaknesses.

Negotiations with the reliable performer can be harrowing. A buyer must concentrate on detail preparation, painstaking need analysis, careful tactical preparation, and firm presentation of objectives. Patience and calm are required, even though the buyer may be easily frustrated when trying to negotiate with this type of person. Outbursts of temper are not the way to succeed in any negotiation. If the buyer uses a combination of need fulfillment and weakness exploitation, success is ensured.

THE LIMITED PERFORMER

The buyer will probably never see a limited performer at the bargaining table. However, this type is always found within any corporation. Since much of the buyer's negotiation goes on inside the company with people in departments other than purchasing, sooner or later he or she will meet a limited performer. This common personality type is characterized by the following basic preferences.

Needs and Weaknesses

Adherence to Standard Operating Procedures

Limited performers live by the book. They strictly adhere to established guidelines and procedures. Any attempt to force them to deviate from procedures causes considerable concern.

Concentration on Detail

Limited performers are quite comfortable handling details.

Security

Security is paramount to limited performers. They usually achieve security by living and operating in a very sheltered environment.

Reaction to outside pressure is generally quite negative. This type of person usually has no desire to assume any authority, to act independently, to take chances, or to make major decisions.

No Sudden Changes

Sudden or abrupt changes are traumatic experiences for limited performers. Change is considered bad by itself, but sudden change is a threatening and fearsome experience.

Group Membership

Limited performers are very insecure and react unfavorably to working alone. They need the constant reassurance that comes from operating as a member of a group. Working within the group spells protection.

Minimum Responsibility

Limited performers are followers, not leaders. They have little desire for responsibility. This type of person is reluctant to delegate to others, and is incapable of facing trouble that requires firm action and risk taking.

Desire for Strong Leadership

Limited performers react favorably to strong leadership and highly respect those who are willing to make decisions, face up to trouble, and take unpopular stands if necessary. This kind of person needs to have the way paved. Such people are incapable of putting themselves forward to break new ground or to seek and develop new relationships with other people or departments. However, if the doors are opened, instructions given clearly, and operational limits defined, they usually work well. The stronger the leadership, the more detailed the instructions, the tighter the environment, and the more precise the work, the better this type of personality will work. The need for the security of a rigidly circumscribed environment is paramount.

Critical of Others

This kind of person tends to be super critical of others, but not to the point of forcing a confrontation. Limited performers feel that no one else can give a task the same attention to detail that they give. They may criticize the lack of attention to minute detail by others, but are otherwise quite diplomatic in handling people. As negotiators they will not defend a position if there is disagreement because they have no stomach for facing opposition. Compliancy is the mark of this type of personality.

As noted, limited performers should never be put at a negotiating table. They cannot handle the give-and-take of a negotiation. They cannot handle ideas that deviate from standard procedures. The necessity for making decisions, taking potentially unpopular stands, assuming authority, dealing with controversy, and facing confrontation at the negotiation table would prove to be their complete undoing. This introverted personality is happy in a restricted environment with protection from the outside world. Delighting in precise activities, they handle detail easily.

While this may not sound like a very productive or even attractive profile of a personality, there is much to be said for this kind of person. Every company needs a certain percentage of limited performers to handle the work that demands extreme accuracy. However, certain precautions must be taken to ensure maximum performance. A strong leader must maintain the protected environment, direct a constant stream of reassurance to this person, and protect him or her from outside distraction or confrontation.

It is not easy to work with a limited performer. The buyer will have difficulties getting opinions on problems from such a person. Under no circumstances should the buyer ever allow this type of person on a negotiating team; that would be a disaster. The limited performer is incapable of making a decision.

There are usually people in every department, including purchasing, with some of the personality traits of a limited performer. It is up to the manager to find the right spot for them so that their talents are used to the best interest of the department and the company. But never let them negotiate!

Buyer Counteractions

While it is unlikely that the buyer will ever confront the limited performer at the bargaining table, such contact is likely in in-house business matters. The buyer must be able to spot this type of person quickly so time is not wasted.

General Strategy and Approach

To negotiate with this type of person, the buyer must *give explanations and more explanations.* The buyer must pay attention to the detail in any proposal presented. If the buyer is fairly precise, he or she may be able to establish some sort of common bond.

The buyer must avoid extreme pressure and outright confrontation. Slow and easy is the path. Although it is often quite frustrating to try to sell an idea or concept under these circumstances, patience is mandatory. Create a nonthreatening atmosphere.

Try to sell the person first on the importance of expanding relationships within the company. The chances of success are inverse to the amount of variance from current standard operating procedures.

If a stalemate is reached and there is no hope that the limited performer will accept the proposition, then there is only one approach left. *Go over the individual's head to the manager.* The person who manages a limited performer will know that all she or he has to do is issue an instruction. There is no doubt that the person will comply with the manager's wishes.

IMPORTANCE OF CEMENTING THE BUYER-SELLER RELATIONSHIP

The buyer's relationship with the supplier depends on the philosophy of the buyer or the company. Many buyers practice a philosophy of careful supplier selection, a programmed supplier development approach, and long-term relationships. This is the prevailing viewpoint of most professional buying staffs. The opposite philosophy—of changing suppliers strictly on the basis of lowest price—still has adherents, but it is a dangerous way of life. Loyalty works both ways; the more comfortable a relationship, the better the possibilities are for a negotiation that will extend the relationship and bring satisfaction to both parties.

The process of need recognition and personality evaluation, discussed in this chapter, can help the buyer maintain the buyer-seller relationship. Some people may consider this unnecessary, since the buyer usually has the true reins of power in terms of the dollar volume involved and his or her option to go elsewhere if no agreement can be reached. However true this may be, the preservation of the relationship between the buyer's company and the supplier should be considered. As has been pointed out, this is becoming more and more important as the marketplace becomes more difficult in terms of supply and cost control.

What the inexperienced buyer often fails to appreciate is the fact that if some care is given to developing a strong relationship, tangible, money-saving benefits may be derived. The supplier can offer a range of services including administrative support, research and development, graphics design, engineering assistance, quick reaction when trouble strikes, and almost any other supportive service needed by the buyer. Granted, the buyer can always demand these assists, and if volume is large enough they will be granted. The secret, however, is in how they are supplied. The colder the relationship, the less energetic the response to the needs of the buyer. The better the relationship, the better the services. If the buyer ever took the time to calculate the cost of these extra services if they were to be performed by the buyer's company, he or she would realize instantly the value of a good supplier.

It is in the interest of buying economics, as well as negotiation ability, that the buyer exert every possible means of cementing the relationship with the supplier. And since relationships are conducted between people, the ability to understand people is a vital part of the negotiator's job.

SUMMARY

Negotiation is a people-oriented experience. The ability to understand people, their needs, their wants, and their weaknesses is an integral part of the negotiation process.

Before attempting to analyze the personality characteristics of others, the buyer must have an understanding of self that is not easily acquired. An honest self-analysis is most difficult for a person to perform, but it must be done. We must know ourselves before we can presume to know others. Self-analysis is important because it helps shape one's self-image, which in turn will affect expectation levels in regard to future accomplishments.

Once the buyer is aware of his or her own motivational factors, he or she must recognize the attitudes, opinions, emotions, and temperament in others. Since negotiations can be affected by personality traits, needs, and wants, the buyer must learn to "read" people. Knowledge of the personality traits of the opposition is a valuable planning and operational tool in negotiations.

Business is conducted with people and by people, inside and outside of the company. Therefore, the buyer must learn to understand people. This understanding affects not only formal negotiations, but also every aspect of the buyer's career. The inability to handle people will doom the buyer as a negotiator and stunt career growth.

The buyer must be trained to quickly recognize

The power seeker—task-oriented, seeking challenge and opportunity, results-oriented, potentially confrontational, and a good decision maker.

The persuader—people-relating, socially oriented, ambitious and tough under a cloak of amiability, likeable, affable, and a dangerous opponent at the negotiating table.

The reliable performer—solid, dependable, comfortable in supportive surroundings, resistant to sudden change, and dependent on past precedents for confidence in decision making.

The limited performer—lacking in self-confidence, in need of a sheltered environment, nondecisive, introverted, and likely to crack under pressure.

6

Safeguarding
the Agreement

In the United States, transactions involving the sale of goods are covered by the Uniform Commercial Code (UCC) in every state except Louisiana. The provisions covering sales may vary in interpretation by state but must be within the framework of the Code. The Code was designed to impose some order and consistency on the laws governing sales and to give to the buyer stronger warranty protection than that available under common law.

This chapter deals with some of the problems that buyers encounter on a daily basis as they attempt to protect their companies and their agreements. Sellers will try to limit their liability under any agreement.

Basically, there are two types of battles that must be fought. The first battle arises when the purchase order and the acknowledgment forms do not match. The other battle deals with the wording of the terms and conditions on the back of most purchase orders and the protection given to the buyer by these terms and conditions.

Under the old interpretations, if an acknowledgment did not conform completely with the terms of the purchase order, there was no contract, only a counteroffer. However, the UCC has loosened that interpretation to allow an acknowledgment that varies from the terms of the purchase order to act as an acceptance. The criterion seems to be that the variances not materially affect the basic terms of the agreement. When there are substantial differences, additional terms, or disclaimers of warranty, conflicts occur.

Implied warranties are included in every contract of sale as a matter of law and are not the result of specific negotiation on the subject. Although these warranties are great protection for the buyer, they still must be buttressed by negotiation and tight contract language. The buyer must be cognizant of the types of warranties available and of the need to include warranty negotiation in the planning and negotiation process. In most situations, the buyer will find warranty protection to be very important.

Although there will be many times when the warranty is not a matter for negotiation, the buyer must be constantly alert for attempts by sellers to use disclaimer clauses to waive their responsibilities under implied warranties. Such clauses, if unchallenged, may work to the detriment of the buyer.

WARRANTIES

Warranties and disclaimers of warranty are a major problem for the buyer today. The Uniform Commercial Code has acknowledged several types of warranties for the protection of the buyer. However, the parties on the opposite side of a transaction often attempt to circumvent the warranty provisions by a variety of disclaimers. These disclaimers are designed to limit the terms and narrow the liability area that the court would consider in the event of a confrontation.

Warranties of quality under the Code are of three kinds:

1. The express warranty,
2. The implied warranty of merchantability, and
3. The implied warranty of fitness for a particular purpose.

Bear in mind that the basic concept of any warranty is related to quality of the goods. The buyer may expect average quality goods to perform adequately. The buyer cannot expect goods to perform in excess of the basic function for which they were intended.

The *express warranty* is applicable whenever a seller makes any kind of representation by a specific statement of fact as to how the goods will perform. It is important that the express statement on the quality of the goods affected the buyer's decision to purchase them. Express warranties may be either oral or written. If the warranties are oral and are important to the final contract, they must be made a part of the wording on the order or contract; otherwise the Parole Evidence Rule, which prohibits oral testimony, may thwart protection.

The express warranty is created and imposed on the seller by the conditions specified in the contract. There is no set legal wording required for the establishment of an express warranty; the word warranty need not even appear in the document. An express warranty is created whenever the seller expressly guarantees to the buyer some particular quality or characteristic related to the product or material sold.

It is really not the express warranty that carries the weight, but the fact that the parties intended to be bound by the seller's promise regarding certain characteristics of the merchandise. In other words, the buyer considered the warranty the inducement for buying. Warranties may be concerned with specific quality, performance (in the case of equipment), or material specifications. For example, if a buyer gives performance specifications stating that the equipment to be purchased must operate at a given speed or rate of efficiency and the seller accepts the contract, there is an express warranty that the equipment will function according to the performance specifications.

It is not uncommon for vendors to make express warranties in their sales or technical literature. If the buyer relies on these statements and has no adverse knowledge, an express warranty has been created. In questions of enforcement of express warranties in court, cases are usually settled in favor of the buyer.

The implied warranty of merchantability is probably the most important of the warranties to the buyer. Basically it refers to what the buyer can expect to get in terms of the quality of goods being purchased. The buyer is entitled to get goods of fair to average quality. In other words, the buyer can expect and is entitled to goods that perform as the goods were intended to perform. The term "normal standards" is often used to describe the quality that the buyer can expect to receive. Under the Code the buyer gets the warranty of merchantability automatically. The warranty is in force for the term of the agreement unless it is waived or disclaimed and the buyer agrees to the disclaimer. The buyer must be on the watch for attempts by the seller to exclude this warranty from the agreement. This warranty is *vital* to the buyer and it must be preserved intact at all times.

The Uniform Commercial Code covers the point of how much variation there may be between the goods ordered and the goods received. Under Section 2-314 of the Code, there are six minimum requirements for goods to be considered legally merchantable.

Goods to be merchantable must be at least such as:

a. Pass without objection in the trade under the contract description; and
b. In the case of fungible goods, are of fair average quality within the description; and
c. Are fit for ordinary purposes for which such goods are used; and
d. Run, within the variations permitted by the agreement, of even kind, quality, and quantity within each unit and among all units involved; and
e. Are adequately contained, packaged, and labeled as the agreement may require; and
f. Conform to the promises or affirmations of fact made on the container or label, if any.

The implied warranty of fitness for a particular purpose is in force only if it is specifically made part of the agreement—this warranty is not given automatically to the buyer. The necessary elements of this warranty involve communication of the buyer's purpose, reliance on the pronouncements of the seller that the product will perform the particular job, and definite knowledge by the seller that the buyer is relying on the product's performance. Buyers *must* convey their needs clearly to the sellers and then rely on the sellers to deliver the product that will perform the particular task.

DISCLAIMERS

Sellers may attempt to avoid the consequences of warranties through the use of disclaimers. The buyer must make sure that those statements of fact made by the seller that are vital to the agreement are part of the written document characterizing the arrangement. One of the most common devices used by sellers today is called the *merger* or *entireties clause*. The goal of this clause is to eliminate any verbal statements, conditions, promises, or other commitments which the seller or seller's agent might have made to the buyer. The merger clause attempts to make the written agreement the sole evidence of the agreement. This would eliminate any other agreements between the buyer and seller that might have influenced the buyer to make the purchase. A typical merger clause might read:

> This agreement constitutes the final written expression of all of the terms of this agreement and is the complete and exclusive statement of those terms. Any and all representations, promises,

warranties, or oral statements by seller's agent that differ in any respect from the terms of this written agreement shall be given no force or effect.

Although the wording in various agreements may differ, the gist is the same—it is an attempt to limit the liability of the seller. The buyer must be alert for these clauses. If the buyer does not object to such clauses being in an agreement the buyer may find that his or her protection under the Code has been limited.

The merger clause approach is generally used to negate express warranties. However, a different approach is taken in the case of the warranty of merchantability. The disclaimer to this is usually hidden in the seller's form of acceptance. The seller wants to limit vendor liability to a given period of time and restrict the warranty to repair or replacement of materials in which defects are due to materials or workmanship. The following wording is typical of the language found on sellers' forms:

> The seller expressly warrants the goods described herein to be free from all defects due to materials or workmanship for a period of 30 days from the date of delivery. This warranty is in lieu of all other warranties express or implied, including the implied warranty of merchantability.

Buyers must recognize any attempt to negate their warranties and must actively negotiate around the problem. The Uniform Commercial Code requires that a disclaimer be prominent and that it mention the implied warranty of merchantability.

Attempts to get around the warranty of fitness for a particular purpose have no restrictions under the Code. The buyer must be alert for the vendor's attempts to limit warranties and be prepared to negotiate around the disclaimer.

The next logical progression for the seller is to attempt to limit liability with the following clause:

> The parties agree that the buyer's sole and exclusive remedy against the seller shall be for repair or replacement of parts deemed defective due to materials or workmanship as provided herein. The buyer agrees that no other remedy, including, but not limited to, incidental or consequential damages, for any lost profits, lost sales, injury to person or property, or any other incidental or consequential loss, shall be available to the buyer.

This type of clause is usually found along with a disclaimer of warranty of some kind. If buyers permit clauses like this in an agreement, they are at a disadvantage, even though they have retained the warranty of merchantability. The warranty is rendered virtually inactive because the amount of dollar loss for the breach has been severely limited.

When preparing for and conducting any type of negotiation, buyers must be cognizant of their rights in the event of a breach of contract by a seller or controversy over the transaction. It is easier to cover the ground in advance than to try to remedy a bad situation in court.

Remember the basic rule of contracts—if something is important to the buyer, it should be made a part of whatever kind of writing is used to document the agreement.

TERMS AND CONDITIONS— DOMESTIC PURCHASING CLAUSES

Depending on the situation, it may be necessary for the buyer to engage in the negotiation of terms and conditions of the contract. Usually, the terms and conditions related to a given industry and its needs will be found on the reverse side of the purchase order form. However, it is surprising how many firms issue purchase orders without the necessary terms and conditions either on the order form or in an attachment to it.

The terms used in various industries are almost unlimited. The following clauses are suggested because they contain general terms which could be used in almost any industry. Our objective is to provide the buyer with a list of clauses that can safeguard most agreements. *However, it is strongly recommended that the buyer check with legal counsel to confirm that these terms do indeed satisfy the needs of the buyer's company.*

Assignment Clause

The primary purposes for an *assignment clause* forbidding the assignment of the contract, are to protect the buyer and to preserve the relationship with the original contractor. The buyer makes a deal with a given supplier for specific reasons and normally does not want the contract assigned to another party. This wording is suggested:

> Neither this order nor any rights and obligations under it shall be assigned or contracted to third parties by seller without the prior written consent of buyer, and to attempt an assignment otherwise shall cause this agreement to be void.

Terms Clause

A *terms clause* prohibits sellers from injecting any waivers of warranty, or changes in terms, without the consent of the buyer. This wording is suggested:

> This purchase order together with any attached drawings or specifications incorporated herein sets forth the entire terms and conditions, and no other terms and conditions in any document, acceptance, or acknowledgment shall be effective or binding unless expressly agreed to in writing by buyer. Payment for goods specified herein or acceptance of physical delivery thereof shall not constitute acceptance of such goods. All goods received shall be subject to buyer's acceptance or rejection. If rejected, goods or work shall be returned for credit at seller's risk or account; handling and transportation charges, replacement, or modification is at seller's risk and obligation. Any written waiver by buyer of any particular breach or default hereunder by seller shall not constitute a continuing waiver or a waiver of any other breach or default.

Warranty Clause

The *warranty clause* is the clause the buyer should use to establish warranty restrictions and conformation with various state and federal regulations, to remove the seller's ability to restrict and to establish the survival of warranties after delivery. This type of clause is probably the most important one in the contract; it should be carefully written and, if necessary, negotiated. This wording is suggested:

> Seller expressly represents, warrants, and agrees that all goods, equipment, machinery, materials, merchandise, articles, service, or work provided or performed on or off buyer's premises covered by this order will:
> a. Conform in all respects to buyer's specifications, drawings, samples, or other description furnished or supplied or specified by buyer, and where engineered by buyer shall be treated as confidential and subject to requirements hereinafter set forth;
> b. Where of seller's design, of seller's specification, of seller's standard product, or where seller is notified in advance by buyer of the purpose or purposes of intended use, that the same is and will be fit and sufficient for such purpose or purposes;
> c. Conform with all applicable local, state, and federal laws and regulations, and should seller be responsible for installation,

all permits, liaisons, and any other government authorization shall be seller's obligation;

d. Be of good quality, merchantable, of good workmanship, of materials best suited for the intended purposes, and free of defects of any kind;

e. Be, where applicable, in full and strict compliance with:

(1) Fair Labor Standards Act, 1938, as amended.

(2) Standards and regulations of federal and state Occupational Safety and Health Acts, Federal Noise Control Act, and Federal Clean Air Act.

(3) Federal, state, and local food, drug, and cosmetic acts, or similar laws and regulations, as amended.

(4) Equal employment opportunity laws and regulations, pursuant to executive order 11246; Section 202 is acknowledged and incorporated herein by reference, including but not limited to paragraphs (1) through (7) of the contract clause, unless exempted by the provision of Section 201 of said executive order. Seller agrees to provide upon buyer's request a certificate of compliance with Equal Employment Opportunity Act, Employment of the Handicapped Act, and Employment of Vietnam Veterans Act.

(5) Consumer Product Safety Act, as amended, with full notification of compliance to buyer, where applicable hereunder.

(6) Federal Hazardous Substances Act and Federal Poison Prevention Packaging Act, 1970;

f. Not infringe any United States or foreign letters patent, copyrights, or trademarks. If by reason of any patent, copyright, or trademark infringement or charge of unfair competition resulting in any claim, demand, judgment, order, or settlement whereby buyer is prevented or may be prevented from using any article, merchandise, material, service, machinery, or work covered by this purchase order, seller will, at own expense, either procure for buyer the right to continue using the same, replace the same with a similar noninfringing article, merchandise, material, service, machinery, or work satisfactory to buyer, or modify the same in a manner satisfactory to buyer so it becomes noninfringing. Further, seller disclaims any interest in the trademarks, other than its own, utilized in performance of purchases hereunder. Seller agrees it will not use any materials, including rejected goods, such as containers, labels, or cartons bearing any of buyer's trademarks in connection with shipment or sale to any person, firm, or corporation other than buyer except upon written instruction of buyer.

g. Where seller is to supply machinery and/or equipment and/or install same at buyer's facility pursuant to this purchase order,

seller further agrees to indemnify, defend, and hold harmless buyer from and against all liability for damages arising from injuries to person or damage to property arising out of or connected in any way with seller's, and its employees', agents', or servants', performance under buyer's purchase order, and without limiting the generality of the foregoing, any and all expenses, legal or otherwise, including attorneys' fees, which may be incurred by buyer in the defense of any claim action or suit in which such liability may be asserted. Seller shall carry insurance protecting buyer in not less than minimum limits of property damage $1,000,000 and public liability $500,000/$1,000,000, providing buyer's coverage with certificates of insurance from mutually approved insurance companies. Seller agrees that the term "cost," where applicable, shall not include any amount seller shall be required to pay in regard to property damage and public liability insurance which exceeds the amount seller has now or in the future may have in effect.
These warranties and each of them are in addition to any and all warranties pursuant to applicable provisions of the UCC or implied by law. All such warranties survive the delivery of the goods and materials and the receipt thereof by buyer.

Inspection Clause

The *inspection clause* protects the buyer's right to inspect, reject, or partially accept. It also establishes the rights of the buyer and the obligation of the seller in the case of a rejection. The following wording represents a general approach, but should cover the majority of situations:

If the buyer chooses, and the seller agrees, buyer's representatives may go to seller's plant of manufacturing or processing to observe and inspect prior to shipment goods, materials, machinery, articles, merchandise, services, or work performed or to be used in filling this order, and such items not satisfactory or which do not conform to buyer's samples, description, use, or specifications may be rejected. Such an inspection, however, does not preclude buyer from making a further inspection at a later date nor from asserting any claim(s) against seller for breach of any warranties, representations, or agreements. Rejected goods before or after delivery are not replaceable except upon buyer's written order, and all costs relative to rejected goods are the responsibility of seller. Where applicable, seller's obligation to obtain a USDA certificate or other type of inspection certificate is not to be construed to be an exclusive method of inspection. Buyer retains the right to inspect all goods for compliance with purchase order specifications and written amendments hereto.

Equipment and Installation Guaranty

An *equipment and installation guaranty* is a special clause to be used in cases where the seller is to do an installation of equipment. As it is usually written, this is a very strict clause that is heavily in favor of the buyer. Here again, the buyer should notice and attempt to thwart any efforts by the seller to waive liability. A clause like this might have to be negotiated, and the going might be rough. However, if the buyer feels the need to have such a clause, the effort is worthwhile. The following wording is suggested:

> Any usage statement, guaranty, or warranty stated in seller's quotation relating to equipment, materials, service, or work will be superseded either by terms and conditions stated on the face of this purchase order or in their absence by the following seller's statement:
>
> a. If said equipment, material, service, or work, which is found to be defective in workmanship, material, or design (except where of buyer's design) fails or is found to be nonconforming with specifications within 18 months after shipment or 12 months after date of putting same into service, whichever date occurs first, it shall at buyer's option be repaired in place by seller or be replaced at buyer's facility by seller or be returned at seller's expense (including transportation and handling costs) for full refund.
>
> b. All items delivered or supplied hereunder will be free and clear of all liens, encumbrances, claims, and security interest of whatever nature, and buyer may withhold payment pending receipt of evidence in form and substance satisfactory to it of the absence of such liens, encumbrances, claims, and security interest.
>
> In the event buyer's technical personnel or other representatives should issue advice, approvals, or instructions, it shall be deemed an expression of personal opinion only and shall not affect buyer's or seller's rights and obligations unless the same is set forth in an amendment to the purchase order signed by an authorized representative of the buyer's purchasing department.

Buyer's Property Clause

The *buyer's property clause* is designed to protect the proprietary rights of the buyer where the buyer has either supplied, designed, or paid for tools, plates, artwork, or similar items. There has been a considerable amount of controversy in past years, particularly in the packaging industry, over the ownership of films and plates, sometimes even when the buyer has paid for the items. The rationale proposed by sellers in these cases is vague, but it seems to center around the fact that they have contributed technical skills and expertise in the preparation of these items and thus have a proprietary interest. Naturally, the buyers do not share this opinion. The following clause is worded to eliminate any doubts:

> All materials, tools, plates, artwork, film, drawings, specifications, and other information (designated simply as "data") furnished or paid for by buyer shall be clearly identified as buyer's property and handled as a confidential matter with no publicity or promotional activity and used only in behalf of buyer and in the fulfillment of this purchase order, unless seller obtains buyer's written consent to do otherwise.

Indemnity Clause

An *indemnity clause* is a somewhat standard hold harmless clause that is found in almost every piece of boilerplate wording on a purchase order. The particular format offered here goes a little further than the standard clause, for it covers the issuance of insurance policies to protect the buyer. An interesting addendum here is the granting of the right to the buyer's company to undertake its own defense at its option. This approach is prevalent with the food industry, in which firms often prefer to handle complaints themselves in accordance with company policy. This, again, is a tough clause that could become the center of some heated negotiation but is valuable to the buyer. The suggested wording is as follows:

> Seller agrees to reimburse, indemnify, defend, protect, pay costs and attorneys' fees and expenses, and save harmless buyer, its successors, assigns, and customers or users of its products, for any and all injuries, losses, damages, claims, demands, settlements, suits, or actions in law, equity, or otherwise and for obligations to pay, including loss of production time arising as a result of the sale or use of the materials, merchandise, equipment, articles, services, or work covered by the purchase order and arising out of the breach of any representation, warranty, or agreement contained herein or arising out of any warranty implied by law, including without being limited to demands, claims, orders, decrees, or regulations of any government body, commission, or agency.
>
> Seller further agrees that it will, upon demand, obtain and pay for insurance policies protecting buyer against such losses as heretofore stated in such amounts as buyer may from time to time request with mutually agreed on insurance companies, and seller shall forthwith send to buyer certificates of insurance indicating full compliance.

Buyer shall, at its option, have the right to undertake the defense, handling, or settlement of all actions, claims, or demands against it, arising in whole or in part out of any breach of warranty (expressed or implied), misrepresentation, or breach of agreement, and seller agrees to reimburse buyer for all investigative expenses and legal costs, attorneys' fees, other fees, costs, and disbursements arising from seller's breach of warranty, misrepresentation, or breach of other agreement hereunder; buyer retains the right in such event to cancel this order either before or after delivery, in whole or in part, and return goods to the seller, and receive back the purchase price, freight in and out, and all packing charges.

Delivery Clause

The *delivery clause* sets out the importance of meeting delivery schedules and clearly establishes remedies for failure to perform. The following wording is suggested:

Time is of the essence for this purchase order. If seller fails to make delivery as scheduled by buyer or fails to perform the services at the time agreed upon or fails to perform services so as to endanger its ability to make timely delivery or timely performance of service, buyer reserves the right to cancel, purchase elsewhere, and hold seller accountable for additional costs or damages incurred by buyer. It is further agreed that buyer shall not be held liable and may return to seller at seller's expense, including freight both ways, materials, merchandise, equipment, articles, service, or work manufactured, processed, or delivered in excess of this order.

Count and Weight Clause

A *count and weight clause* is needed where the payment owed for materials is determined by scale weight. The intent is to develop a standard procedure to eliminate arguments over scale weights. The following wording is suggested:

Buyer's count and weight will be accepted as final and conclusive on all shipments.

Party Clarification Clause

The *party clarification clause* is intended to clarify who the parties to an agreement are. Often, this type of clause is the opening paragraph of an agreement. Regardless of where it appears, it is essential to the agreement to avoid confusion. It may be worded like this:

> The name _____ as used here shall mean
> (abbreviated)
> _____, its subsidiaries,
> (full name)
> affiliates, successors, or assigns.

Applicable Law Clause

The intent of the *applicable law clause* is to establish what state's law shall apply in the event that a controversy develops and the parties go to court. The reason this can be an issue is that the UCC has been interpreted differently in various states. Each company's department will want to be in court in the state where the atmosphere is the most conducive to a settlement in its favor. Moreover, the question of jurisdiction can become a factor unless the state is specified, especially where the companies involved are in different states. The suggested wording is as follows:

> This contract shall be construed and accepted in accordance with the laws of the state of _____.

Modification Clause

The intent of a *modification clause* is to give the buyer some latitude to make modifications in the agreement without creating a situation of breach of contract. This type of clause might be worded like this:

> Buyer may, upon reasonable notice, modify any term or condition of this contract, including the specifications, quantities, or delivery dates. The seller, upon receipt of a written change notice, shall promptly proceed to make the indicated changes.

Cancellation Clause

No contract or agreement should be written without including a clear *cancellation clause*. The particular example given here goes beyond the normal cancellation clause and spells out the obligations and actions required of the seller. The suggested wording is this:

> Buyer reserves the right to cancel this order in whole or in part at any time by written notice to seller, in the event such termination

is otherwise than for default of seller. Such termination shall be effective in the manner specified in said notice. Seller shall immediately discontinue work and the placing of orders and, where applicable, the shipping of orders for materials and supplies in connection with the performance of said order. The extent of compensation or reimbursement, if any, shall be negotiated between buyer and seller on a fair, just, and equitable basis, provided, however, that nothing in this item shall abrogate the right of buyer to cancel and/or excuse seller's failure to comply with terms and conditions of this order.

The foregoing pieces of contractual language will forestall almost all of the potential problems of any agreement. It may be necessary, for certain types of agreements, to go much farther afield. One such instance would be an agreement for construction of a building. This is a completely different situation from the usual industrial agreement; it should be given special handling with the assistance of the legal department.

CLAUSES FOR PURCHASING OVERSEAS

With the expanding need for overseas procurement in many industries, buyers are placed in the position of having to be very careful in setting up agreements. The following considerations are a must for any buyer contemplating purchases from foreign suppliers. The wide variation in the laws of other countries makes it impossible to develop a standard set of purchase order terms that will fit all situations. The buyer should check with legal counsel both domestically and in the country in question before drafting a final version. Proper wording to ensure application of purchase order terms and conditions is essential. The following are important considerations in this process:

1. When preparing an agreement, the buyer should make sure it is reviewed by competent legal counsel before using it. This ensures that all necessary protective aspects have been covered.

2. Before finalizing an agreement, the buyer is advised to get the supplier to accept the jurisdiction of United States courts. This is highly desirable and should be done in advance of signing the agreement. It should be pointed out that this acceptance is usually seen as a part of the normal course of doing business and is usually not much of a problem to obtain.

3. Prior to signing, the buyer should determine whether or not the seller has any assets in the United States. This can be done by asking the seller to list United States holdings, by having the buyer's company's banker check, or by utilizing the Dun and Bradstreet service, which concentrates on this aspect of international business.

4. If the seller refuses to accept the jurisdiction of the United States courts, the buyer should try to negotiate the inclusion of an arbitration clause along these lines:

    Any controversy, disagreement or claim arising out of, or relating to, this contract or to the breach of this contract shall be settled by arbitration. Such arbitration shall be in accordance with the rules of the American Arbitration Association, and judgment on the award by the arbitrator(s) may be entered in any court having jurisdiction thereof.

    Special note: If the seller will not agree to accept the jurisdiction of the United States courts, has no assets in the United States, and refuses to agree to settle disputes by arbitration, under no circumstances should any business be conducted.

5. Billing address: The buyer should be sure to state clearly where invoices are to be sent.

6. Packaging instructions: The buyer should be sure to include complete instructions or specifications for packing for shipment. If there is decorative packaging involved, the problem becomes much more complicated. Variations in presses and inks in other countries can result in packaging not up to the standard expected by the buyer. To forestall such problems, the buyer should provide the following preparatory materials for the printer to use:

    - a set of original art complete with color swatches.
    - a complete set of color-separated films.
    - a set of color standards showing the acceptable variances for color range.
    - a set of progressives that indicate the sequence of color laydown. (Sequence of color laydown is vital.)
    - an approved final proof for comparison with what the printer is producing. (This can be produced on a proofing press.)
    - a set of ink samples, preferably small tins of the inks to be used or matched. (If U.S. inks must be used, provide

the manufacturer's name and the ink code numbers needed for ordering.)

7. Quality control: The buyer should clarify what quality control measures are expected of the seller. The buyer should specify the quality control techniques and state the penalties the seller must pay if the material is rejected. For example, the seller must agree to accept the costs of the buyer's obtaining replacements locally if the material is rejected and the buyer's production schedule is thereby endangered.

8. Indemnity: A complete indemnity clause, which covers the buyer in the event of rejection, should be included. One problem that often arises when an advance payment has been made is that of obtaining reimbursement if there is a rejection. This should be covered by requiring that the seller obtain an insurance policy in the amount of the contract and with underwriters located in countries where there is unrestricted transferability of funds. In some countries claims are paid in that country's currency, and sending the funds out of the country is prohibited.

9. Pricing: The buyer should specify whether the prices are to be firm or subject to increase. If they are subject to adjustment, then the formula for determination of the adjustments should be included as part of the contract.

10. Delivery instructions: Delivery instructions should be spelled out in the contracts, including shipping dates, expected delivery dates, and method of shipment, i.e., boat, air, or whatever.

11. Passage of title: When the title to the goods passes should be clearly indicated in the contract. If there is to be any special arrangement as to who is to file damage claims against a carrier, this should also be clarified.

12. Nonassignment clause: This clause is a must if the buyer is to maintain any semblance of control.

13. Materials warranty: This is a standard precaution.

14. Deviations and substitutions: If there is to be an allowance for the seller to make substitutions or to deviate from the specifications, the limits of acceptability must be determined by the buyer and transmitted to the seller.

15. Cancellation clause: The conditions for cancellation by the buyer must be spelled out. There should be a clear definition of the conditions under which the buyer may cancel without

penalty. Points to be considered as adequate reasons for buyer cancellation include seller insolvency, a change in government regulations affecting delivery, currency devaluation, military action or terrorist activities, inability by seller to obtain the proper transportation, strikes, and reassignment of the order in violation of the nonassignment clause.

16. Seller certificate of origin: The buyer should require a certificate of origin on all parts and materials, as a means of determining how the seller is handling the contract.

17. Legal compliance: A clause requiring the seller to comply with all laws that apply to the purchase should be included.

18. Patent protection: The seller must agree to indemnify and hold the buyer free and harmless of all costs, expenses, and damages incurred as a result of either alleged or actual patent infringement.

19. Completeness of the agreement: This clause states that the entire agreement is represented by the purchase order and any other writings involved in the total agreement and that no other communication, written or oral, and no other understanding or proposal, written or oral or implied, is included in the agreement. The purpose of this clause is to preclude the citing of the Parole Evidence Rule for alleged oral agreements, over and above the written agreement, that might waive the liability of the seller. Such a clause also effectively disposes of any future disclaimers.

It is important in dealings with foreign suppliers that extreme care be given to every detail of the transaction. Disputes are hard to settle, so the clearer the document, the less chance there will be of a disagreement. The buyer should use legal counsel every step of the way.

SUMMARY

The contract terms discussed in this chapter are often the subjects of negotiation. The buyer who is aware of the terminology, the intent of the clauses, the implications of not including the protective clauses, and the effects of carelessness in preparing an agreement is well on the way to being an accomplished negotiator.

The buyer must be constantly aware of the implications of the express warranty, the implied warranty of merchantability, and the warranty of fitness for a particular purpose and of attempts by sellers to evade the responsibilities they bear under these warranties. At minimum, the buyer should always check to make sure that the following clauses are included in any agreement: assignment, terms, shipping and delivery, warranty, buyer's property, and indemnity. All protective clauses are important, but these are the key areas that must be protected.

7

Conduct of the Negotiation

This chapter looks at the actual conduct of the negotiation—the culmination of all of the planning described in preceding chapters. It is not our intent to set rigid rules to be slavishly followed time after time, but to provide guidelines, suggestions, and warnings of things to avoid. We have attempted to present in straightforward terms an overall view of the process of negotiation which the buyer can use as a planning assist, as a checklist to ensure completeness of preparation, and as a warning system for traps and pitfalls. Many commonly asked questions will be answered in a logical sequence.

Before entering into a discussion of the conduct of a negotiation, let us review briefly the purpose of a negotiation. A negotiation between a buyer and a seller is conducted with the purpose of reaching an agreement, usually on a wide variety of subjects. If the negotiation is conducted in the proper spirit, both parties should leave the table reasonably well pleased with the results. The end results depend to a great extent on the philosophy of the buyer and his or her desire to further or inhibit the growth of the relationship between the buyer and the seller. Each party wants something from the other.

If there were no needs to be filled, there would be no reason for a negotiation. The prevailing philosophy is the win-win approach, which says that each party should gain a reasonable amount of satisfaction from the experience. This does not preclude one party from winning more than the other. The purpose of this chapter is to ensure that the buyer comes away with the greater share of concessions.

WHERE TO HOLD THE NEGOTIATION

There are several schools of thought on where negotiations should be held, and each has legitimate arguments. Actually, there is no "school solution" to the question. Much depends on the circumstances, such as the strength or weakness of the buyer's position, the availability of adequate meeting space at a given location, and the general relationship between the parties. Assuming that the situation is fairly normal, the first choice of location has to be the office of the buyer.

Buyer's Office or Location

There are practical as well as psychological advantages in having the negotiation on home ground. The setting is comfortable, familiar, and secure. In addition, the opposition is in strange territory and may feel some tension and uncertainty, which could give the buyer a small initial edge.

The really important factor is that the buyer has all the resource material close at hand. If there is any need to research a point, access to data is relatively easy. This is a significant advantage for the buyer.

Working on the home ground also gives the buyer an opportunity to establish the atmosphere for the negotiation. Since appearances of power can be engineered on the home court, the buyer can, in effect, do some modest intimidation before the meeting starts.

As in all cases, however, there are two sides to the situation. Negotiating on the buyer's ground gives the seller the perfect out if he or she needs or desires to break off the negotiations. Since the seller is cut off from the vendor's data base, he or she can gracefully withdraw at any time. This option is valuable if the seller is feeling pressured. For instance, the seller might be forced into a concession if persistent pressure were applied and he or she had no legitimate way to back away from the issue. Being away from home is the perfect escape hatch for the seller.

Nonetheless, it is still recommended that the buyer, if possible, conduct the majority of negotiations on familiar ground in order to take advantage of all of the amenities and the psychological boost provided by the buyer's location.

The Seller's Office

In those cases where the buyer is in a disadvantageous position or is not really ready to negotiate but has been forced into it, we recommend that the negotiations take place at the seller's location.

The logic is the same—to have a face-saving means for withdrawal. One cannot fight for time on home ground: there is no legitimate reason for a delay, and so the use of such a tactic would reveal the weakness of the buyer's position.

Meeting at the seller's location can also reflect supreme confidence on the part of the buyer. When the buyer takes the initiative with this surprise move, it can create some apprehension on the seller's side. The seller has to wonder why the buyer chose to negotiate in the enemy camp. There will always be a lingering doubt in the seller's mind as to the real reason the buyer chose to emigrate to unfriendly territory. If the buyer is an aggressive personality and full of confidence, such a tactic can help him or her gain an initial advantage.

Because there is so much psychology in negotiations affecting the power balance between the parties, a surprise move often can shift the power balance quickly. This shift can obviate any advantage the seller might have gained by being on home ground.

There are some other factors the buyer should be aware of when dealing on the seller's home ground. If the buyer and seller have a very friendly relationship, it could be to the buyer's disadvantage to work in the seller's backyard. The atmosphere may be too friendly, which would make it hard for the buyer to be as aggressive as normal. Sellers may entertain the buyer, which might "defang" the buyer in future negotiations. The buyer should keep the relationship in perspective and bear in mind that the vendor must be kept at arm's length at all times in negotiation. Losing determination or becoming too sympathetic to the seller's problems will result in the buyer's losing the negotiation.

There is one place where negotiations should *never* take place—at a seller's recreational facility. The atmosphere is all wrong. The buyer, once there, is definitely under obligation to the seller, which is not the way to try to negotiate. Things are tough enough without this extra burden.

Neutral Ground

There are times when it is advisable for the parties to meet in a neutral spot. For instance, if there is a particularly difficult problem to negotiate, the site can have an effect on how the negotiations proceed. If the buyer and seller are antagonistic, the seller will definitely be more wary, more hostile, and more reluctant to concede if forced into negotiating on the buyer's ground. When there is tension prior to a negotiation, the buyer should do everything possible to defuse the situation, including choosing neutral ground.

Sometimes the buyer might use a neutral location in order to get away from the interruptions incurred at the home office. The buyer might also use a neutral site to establish a particular psychological atmosphere. Since the buyer chooses the neutral site, he or she has full control of the entire atmosphere in which the negotiations will be held.

Choosing the Best Site

An analysis of the type of atmosphere desired should be a part of the planning process. The buyer, knowing the personalities of those on the seller's team, can best decide how and where the most advantages will be gained. The combination of personalities and general situation should determine the site, as the following case studies illustrate.

CASE STUDY 1: The buyer is faced with a very dominant personality across the table. The buyer's position is generally strong, yet the supplier is vital to the buyer. There are some difficult points to work out that will probably lead to confrontations during the negotiations. Where should the parties negotiate?

Here is the classic case where the buyer must weigh the potential impact of the personalities involved, the value of the relationship, the monetary impact of the contract, and the need for psychological advantage.

The buyer should, in this type of situation, take full advantage of the strength and security of home base. There is no need for the buyer to become overly concerned about injuring the sensibilities of the seller, since the seller will have little concern for this factor. The more difficult the impending negotiation, the more the buyer will need to bolster his or her position prior to the start of the proceedings. The home site provides a secure base and ensures an initial advantage for the buyer. When dealing with a power seeker, take any advantage possible.

CASE STUDY 2: There is definite hostility between the parties. Personality-wise, the leader of the seller's team is people-oriented, but the leader is also skilled and can be very difficult if pressured to an extreme. The buyer desires to preserve the relationship, but must extract some costly concessions from the seller.

This is not an unusual scenario. Here, the buyer must do everything possible to create a soothing, tranquil atmosphere for the meeting. Handling the seller's personality will not be a difficult matter for the buyer; the problem lies in the potentially explosive subject. This is the type of situation where the slow and easy approach seems to obtain maximum concessions. Therefore, the site should be a neutral one, preferably very comfortable, where some social amenities can be observed. The goal is to have a peaceful setting with no interruptions so the buyer can adopt an easy, relaxed approach.

The selection of the site for a negotiation is not always a simple matter. The shrewd negotiator should be aware of the nuances of every situation. In planning a negotiation, the buyer must consider the situation, the relationship, the expected difficulties, potentially hostile reactions, and the economic impact of the needed concessions. Site selection is affected by all of these factors.

THE NEGOTIATION ROOM

The physical setup of the negotiating room is important. First of all, there should be two rooms, particularly if team negotiation is involved. There should be a main room and a caucus room.

The caucus room is a separate room available for use by either side. Its purpose is to provide a place of respite where private discussions can take place during the negotiation. The room should be close to the main room and equipped with liquid refreshments, a blackboard or easel, pencils, note pads, a table, and comfortable chairs.

The main room should be comfortable, with good lighting and visual aids, such as a blackboard or easel. Recording devices should not be available unless agreed to beforehand by both parties. Experience indicates that recording devices inhibit both sides. People seem to be reluctant to talk freely when the devices are present.

Table Shape

There are no rules about table shape. Often people have to "make do" with what is available at the site. Tables can be round, square, or rectangular. Sometimes the buyer may choose to use no table at all.

Seating Arrangements

There are some options with seating arrangements too. The conventional approach is to allocate one side of the table to each party. This has some disadvantages because it permits each side to develop a feeling of strength and security from the proximity of all the team members. It also enhances communication among team members. The worst characteristic of this arrangement is that it erects an instant barrier, unseen but real in every dimension. The placing of a table between the negotiating parties usually creates an element of tension, which is subconsciously perceived by all present.

An alternative approach is to set up a random seating arrangement that separates team members. This can be somewhat tricky because it may appear to be a bold attempt to intimidate the other side. Such a seating arrangement also hampers communication among team members. With random seating, the buyer must develop a fairly complicated system of signal communication in order to transmit instructions and generally control the team. A primary hazard is loss of control of the negotiation. Control is essential with a team—anything that endangers that control must be handled with great care.

The third alternative is not to use a table at all. This approach is excellent if the buyer wants to set a relaxed atmosphere, but can lead to some control problems. Since it is more difficult to use this technique if there are relatively large numbers of people involved, we do not suggest it for large groups. However, if the negotiating group is small and if the relationship between the parties is friendly, we recommend this approach. The evident informality immediately sets the tone for the entire process. Under certain circumstances and with certain individuals, this is very effective.

Whatever the seating arrangement chosen, it should never be left to chance. Seating arrangement, room setting, and the selection of a caucus room are all part of the planning process for the negotiation. These administrative matters can affect the success or failure of the negotiating process.

Once administration has been adequately dealt with, the stage is set for two major happenings—the preparation of the negotiation plan and the execution of that plan.

DEVELOPING THE "GAME PLAN"

Previous chapters covered the preparatory steps of setting objectives, evaluating the potential positions of the supplier, deciding whether to use the team approach, finalizing planning, and collecting background data. It is now time for the final preparations—the evaluation of one's relative power position, and the choice of the strategy, and the selection of tactics to be used. Whether it is a team or a one-on-one negotiation, the basic approach is the same.

The following discussion is intended to give the buyer a feel for the basic considerations of a plan of action. Depending on individual preference, issue complexity, number of people involved, and time constraints, all factors mentioned may not come into play. However, our objective is to prepare the buyer for the future by providing comprehensive guidelines so the buyer can make sure no important factor is omitted.

THE BASICS OF POWER

The buyer's evaluation of the relative power levels is the starting place for the development of the "game plan." The power relationship will affect overall strategy and the type of tactics employed. The buyer must understand the foundation for a power base. Power can come from a variety of sources. For example:

1. Power comes from knowledge. The more knowledge a buyer has and can project, the more power he or she engenders. Knowledge creates respect, and respect translates into power.

2. Power comes from the buyer's reputation, which is also related to respect. An immaculate reputation based on knowledge, fair dealing, and concern for people and companies enables the buyer to project an image of power.

3. Power is gained by economic factors. The size of the account and its importance to the seller are reflected in the perception of power by both sides. The rewards available in the relationship, be they tangible or intangible, are the basis of power.

4. Power is gained by the threat to monetary gains. The buyer has the power to exercise threats to the well-being of the supplier. On the other hand, the seller has the same capability. Every business transaction has the potential for someone to lose something of value. The buyer must know what options are available if the negotiation fails. If the supplier is the sole source of an item, the buyer's power may be limited. The threat of such an undesirable happening is a facet of power.

5. Power is affected by the standards under which a society operates. Each organized society has its own system of laws, civil procedures, customs, and regulatory restrictions. Within corporations there is the restrictive effect of company policies, which often act as a power base for the negotiator.

6. Power is developed through competition. The competitive forces in the marketplace greatly affect the respective power positions of buyers and sellers.

7. Power is built when there is commitment. With commitment comes loyalty, friendship, dedication, and interest in the needs and plans of others. Business is built on a basis of commitment to the long-range needs of all parties. If there is no commitment, the relationship will most certainly fail.

8. Power is related to security. There is always uncertainty in life, and in business as well. It takes courage to face risks and uncertainty. The introduction of uncertainty into a negotiation or a relationship creates a risk factor that may not be acceptable to the other party.

9. Power rests in the relative capability of parties to negotiate. In short, power will lie with the person who has the greater ability to perform in the negotiation arena. Sheer ability is power.

10. Power comes from position or status. The rank of a person can become a power factor in a negotiation. It is always wise to have the highest ranking purchasing person at a major negotiation. A wise supplier will always come with rank to the bargaining table.

In general, these are the basics of the origins and development of power in almost every situation where a bargain must be struck. These power factors apply to personal relationships as well as business situations.

When evaluating the power levels of the parties, the buyer should consider three questions:

"What is my perception of my power?"

"What does the supplier see my position to be?"

"How do I want the supplier to perceive my power?"

The answer to the first question is buried in the mass of information already developed in preparation for the negotiation. In reviewing the data, the buyer will begin to get a picture or conception of the power levels.

The second question is usually answered by the buyer's list of potential objectives for the supplier. The industry analysis, coupled with information gained throughout the year in conversations with the supplier, generally gives an indication of the seller's concept of the power relationship. The supplier analysis, discussed in Chapter 4, should show the supplier's attitude in the key areas of general response to the buyer, emergency responses, delivery and quality record, and past performance in negotiations.

The answer to the third question is not developed at an instant's notice but is built up over a period of time. When beginning a relationship, the buyer must determine what kind of an image is to be projected. People's perceptions of an individual have a great deal to do with their estimation of the power of that individual in a given situation. In short, the buyer must determine early in the relationship how his or her power base is to be developed and recognized by the seller. The buyer's attitude, knowledge of the industry, reputation, personality, and ability to make sound decisions will determine how powerful the seller perceives the buyer to be.

Bear in mind that while the buyer is trying to project power. the supplier may well be attempting to do the same thing. And what better way is there for a supplier to build a positive concept of power in the mind of the buyer than through outstanding performance? Outstanding suppliers are few and far between and are treasured by buyers. Buyers are often willing to concede to a prime supplier rather than risk losing the supplier. The supplier can virtually erode the buyer's power base through exemplary performance.

Once the buyer has determined power levels, he or she can develop the strategy for the negotiations.

STRATEGY

Strategy is the overall approach to the negotiation. Strategy takes into account the important objectives established and the achievement levels set for those objectives. It is the plan for achieving those objectives. In developing the strategic plan, the buyer should consider the following items.

Objectives

The buyer should review objectives one more time to determine whether any factors that have come up since the objectives were set and ranked change either the approach to or the importance of an objective. In the planning for the conduct of the negotiation, the schedule of introduction of the various objectives is important.

The order of introduction of the objectives is a matter of personal choice. There are no rules to govern this point. Some people prefer to start the negotiation with relatively minor objectives. The idea is to develop a pattern of concession on the part of the seller. Once the pattern is set and there is movement in the negotiation, the buyer can bring up the really important points.

Other people prefer to jump in immediately with a major objective. The rationale in this case is that, by forcing the supplier to come to grips with a key issue immediately, the buyer establishes an element of control. Actually, this is not a bad idea. Most negotiations start off rather slowly, with everyone reluctant to lay anything on the table. The straightforward approach contains an element of surprise and can be effective in achieving a quick concession. There is no particular danger here, because if the seller appears to be reluctant to consider an issue, the buyer can back off and come back to the point at a later time.

In essence, the setting of an agenda, at least for the buyer, ensures that all of the objectives are in their proper place and that none will be overlooked. How the objectives are approached is a matter for the buyer to determine, at least initially. Once into the negotiation, the actions of the seller may determine what objectives will be handled and when. If the negotiation process forces a change in the order, there is really no problem. The important point is that the buyer did have a strategic plan which ensured that all items would receive consideration.

The Opening Approach—Who Talks First

In any negotiation, the opening statement is important for setting the tone for the entire operation. As usual, there are two distinct schools of thought on this subject. One school advocates seizing the opportunity to make the opening remarks. This creates some initial pressure on the supplier and gives the buyer an opportunity to set the stage for future events.

The opening statement can do a number of things for the buyer. It can set an atmosphere that ensures a modicum of tranquillity. It can give the buyer a chance to sell some of his or her philosophy about the buyer-seller relationships. It can help the buyer create a favorable power balance. The buyer achieves this by indicating, even obliquely, that the buyer's team has researched the situation and probably knows the major objectives of the seller. This has a dual effect. It establishes the fact that there is knowledge on the buyer's side, and it gives the buyer a psychological advantage through the element of surprise.

If the buyer does make the opening remarks, he or she should take care not to reveal too much of the buyer's position. The objective is to put the seller on the defensive at once, not to reveal the buyer's cards. Whether or not to make the opening statement depends on the personality and general feeling of confidence of the buyer.

The other approach is to use the tactic of silence and force the seller to begin talking. Silence is a good tactic, mainly because the average negotiator in the United States does not know how to cope with it. Most people cannot abide silence. They become uneasy, restless, on edge, and eventually garrulous. If the seller can be forced into talking immediately, several things may happen. The seller may prematurely disclose his or her position. He or she is almost certain to reveal a lot of information that will help the buyer to determine how well prepared he or she is for the negotiation. In all probability, new information will come out; this is excellent for the buyer. Forcing the sellers to take the initiative may upset their game plan as well. The secret is patience on the part of the buyer. Wait them out, smile, be courteous, be friendly, and keep your own counsel.

No matter which approach is chosen, the choice should be made in the advance planning. The buyer should never go into the negotiation without having decided who is going to make the opening statement. In any event, the buyer should have an opening statement ready for presentation, if the situation dictates. To fail to do so may well result in the loss of the initiative, which sometimes is hard to regain.

TACTICAL PLANNING

Tactics are the maneuvers and actions chosen to implement a strategy. A negotiation maneuver is an action taken to permit the accomplishment of an objective. Negotiation techniques can be determined in advance, as part of the planning process, or they may be chosen as a given situation arises. The following useful techniques are suggested.

Agendas

An agenda is used to establish a sense of control in the negotiation. It should cover, in general terms, the areas up for discussion, without giving away any information on objectives. The agenda provides the buyer's first chance to deliver a message to the other side. An agenda can function as a smoke screen or it can tie in with other maneuvers that may be going on at some time in the session. The buyer can keep things on track by using the agenda or unsettle the other side by making continuous digressions from it.

Remember that the idea is to control the action. Keeping to or departing from the agenda has a psychological impact.

Questions

The asking of questions is a time-honored technique that has a definite place in negotiations. Questions may be used to actually seek information, to avoid answering a question, to stall for time, or just to be controversial.

Questions fall into several categories.

The direct question, which is addressed to a specific person and requires an answer, forces the other party to make some kind of response. The type of response or lack of response can be very revealing to the buyer.

The leading question forces the other side to take some sort of position on a subject. It is a pressure device, useful in pushing matters along.

The provocative question is both valuable and potentially dangerous. Such a question tends to evoke an emotional and often hostile response, which can engender a confrontation. Normally, confrontation should be avoided unless the decision is made to deliberately provoke in order to create the expected response.

The "yes or no" question is an attempt to force the other side into a decision posture. Reluctance to answer may initiate a stalemate, at least temporarily.

If the buyer is on the receiving end of questions he or she can relay the questions to other members of the team. This allows the buyer to gain thinking time or defer the answer to a team member with special expertise.

Questioning is a legitimate tactic that should be used throughout the negotiation.

Concessions

The concession is a powerful bargaining tool, if used wisely. The concession is used to determine what the seller really wants, the extent of the seller's desire for a particular want, and what he or she is willing to give up to achieve that desire. Remember, the seller is playing the same game—trying to determine the extent of the buyer's needs and wants.

The idea behind the concession is for the buyer to give up as little as possible in order to gain a concession of greater value. The preparation of minor tradeable objectives makes sense. There are certain basic rules that must be kept in mind when one is handling concessions in order to avoid mistakes.

1. *Always attempt to have the other side make the first concession.* Although there are several reasons for this, the main one is the psychological advantage of obtaining the first breakthrough. The first concession affects the power balance between the parties.

2. *Always set your aspiration level high.* Do not fall into the trap of assuming that your level is high enough. There are no rules restricting the demands the buyer can make. Better to have aspirations too high than not high enough. If you find that you are achieving your objectives with relative ease, your aspiration level was incorrect. When this happens, the buyer has in effect sold out to the opposition and has failed even more drastically than if some high goals had not been achieved in full measure. Low aspirations lose negotiations.

3. *Never accept the initial offer on a major point.* Usually sellers are prepared to make some concessions. No one really expects the first offer to be accepted. Of course, there will be times when immediate acceptance on a minor point will be beneficial in setting a climate of agreement—this is strictly a judgment decision for the buyer.

4. *Never give anything without getting something in return.* If a concession is obtained, be grateful, accept with alacrity, and be instantly on the lookout for the potential consequences of the concession. However, do not feel that it is necessary to grant a concession in return. It is quite fair not to give a concession in return, and it is good for economic self-preservation.

5. *Never give any concession without being fully aware of the economic and tactical consequences of the act.* Concessions affect the power balance between the parties because they impact on the aspiration levels of the parties. Concessions given too easily can swing the balance of power and the momentum to the other side. Confidence or aspiration level is so important in the negotiation process that any action which tends to affect it must be handled with care and forethought.

6. *Try never to make the first concession on important issues.* The pattern of success or failure seems to be related to concessions on major objectives. Experiments run through the years have shown that the first party to concede on a major objective usually ends up losing the negotiation. Whether or not this is true can be left up to conjecture. What is true is that the first concession on a major issue will severely affect the power balance and aspiration levels of the parties. Always know the consequences of a concession.

7. *The pattern of concessions reflects the ability and resolve of the buyer.* The more determined the buyer, the more frugal the concessions will be. This is not to say that the buyer should never give a concession. This would be foolish. Negotiation is supposed to be a process of reasoned give-and-take, where the parties attempt to reach a mutually satisfactory agreement. A buyer's inability or refusal to make concessions would destroy the negotiation process. But, make concessions where the gain outweighs the loss.

8. *Never reply to a high demand with a counteroffer.* The buyer should handle a high demand by requesting that the seller reduce the demand before any further discussion. By making a high demand, the seller is attempting to trap the buyer into making a counteroffer. If the buyer were to make a counteroffer, it probably would be accepted, because the seller would have realized an aspiration higher than that originally anticipated.

9. *Hoard concessions.* Each concession should bring the buyer closer to a goal or objective. To waste concessions is to lose track of the mission, which is to achieve as many objectives as possible at the maximum level. Concessions are a tool to be used sparingly and wisely. The buyer must always keep track of the number of concessions by each side. Scorekeeping on concessions will indicate whether your concession pattern is reasonable or excessive.

10. *All concessions are tentative until the buyer decides to make them final.* This concept should be made clear to the other side and be made part of the bargaining technique. This concept may grate on one's "sense of fair play," but negotiation is not a sporting event. It is serious business where economic gain or loss can spell success or disaster in the future. Any tactic that is not illegal or morally repugnant is acceptable. The right to change one's mind should remain a viable option

until all agreements have been made final and the agreement has been signed by both parties.

In planning the conduct of the negotiation, the buyer should list concessions desired and concessions that might be given. Planning makes it easier to keep score. The following list of concessions that the buyer might seek is designed to be a thought stimulator and a planning aid. It is not a final list of desirable concessions, because each situation will engender its own list. However, this list will give some clues to the types of concessions that are fair game in a negotiation.

CONCESSIONS THE BUYER MIGHT SEEK

1. Price reductions on a finished item or on a raw material.
2. Various methods of stocking materials or finished goods at the vendor's.
3. Consignment programs where the buyer's company would accept shipments into its plant and pay for the items as they were used. Consignment has been used in the retail business for many years and is now beginning to appear in the industrial marketplace. It works well where an item or material is used heavily and at a fairly predictable level.
4. Packaging concessions such as:
   a. Standardized units for easier in-plant handling.
   b. Special markings on units to facilitate inventory control.
   c. Packaging units designed to facilitate stacking in buyer's plant.
   d. Terms and conditions for utilizing reusable packaging, such as returnable drums, corrugated master containers, reusable pallets, and the like.
   e. No deposit on certain types of packaging where a deposit has been the usual procedure, i.e., for cylinders.
5. Presetting a delivery schedule over a time period.
6. Equalization or absorption of freight.
7. Change in terms. Extended terms are useful when the cost of money is high. There are all sorts of possibilities in this area, ranging from extended payment terms to delayed billing.
8. Improvement in the warranties.
9. Increase in vendor participation in research and develop-

ment, sales promotion assistance, or possibly graphic design help for packaging.

10. Improvement in quality or quality control techniques.

11. Total or partial acceptance of tooling expense or at least a plan for prorating the expense over a lengthy period.

12. Prototype models at no cost or shared cost.

13. Price protection for a given period of time.

14. Long-term contract or use of a blanket order–release order approach.

15. Simplified billing procedures, such as billing once a month.

16. A systems contracting arrangement, if appropriate.

17. Leasing of equipment, instead of buying.

18. Special freight allowances in the event of pickup with the buyer's trucks.

19. Special discounts over and above the industry norm in cases of extra volume, runs during the seller's slack season, or any other special consideration by the buyer to alleviate a strain on the supplier.

These are only a few of the possible concessions that the buyer might seek in a negotiation. The possibilities are limited only by the imagination and knowledge of the buyer. Do not be reluctant to seek such concessions.

The buyer may also elect to offer concessions in order to achieve concessions from the supplier on other issues. Some concessions may benefit the supplier greatly and, at the same time, place the buyer in a commanding position with the seller.

CONCESSIONS THE BUYER MIGHT OFFER

1. Financial assistance for good but financially insecure suppliers. This type of program is used quite often to bolster a supplier with cash-flow problems. The technique usually includes either quick payment of invoices, advances to cover purchase of raw materials, outright loans, joint venturing on a given project, or, possibly, purchase of an interest in the seller's company.

2. Technical assistance to a seller in need of such help. This is a valuable concession that obligates the seller.

3. Agreement to tailor purchases to the most economical production units for the seller.

4. Agreement on a reasonable overrun allowance. This is particularly important in dealings with a packaging supplier.

5. Development of a realistic escalator/de-escalator clause for raw materials based on the contribution of the material to the total cost of the item.

6. Development of a simplified system for verifying and allowing increases in labor costs in a contract (usually a clause geared to the peculiarities of a given industry).

7. Tie-in of advertising for the buyer and seller.

8. Purchase of raw materials by the buyer for conversion into the buyer's product. This works when the buyer is in a position to make a raw material purchase in a volume that normally is not possible for the seller.

9. Permission for the seller to use the buyer's patents or formulas.

10. Relief from specifications when the relief will not result in a product unacceptable to the buyer.

Giving and receiving concessions is at the heart of the negotiation process. How the concessions are planned and executed will determine the success of the process. When a concession is given or received, the negotiators must be sure to weigh the effect of the concession on the point at hand, as well as on the entire negotiation. The ability to use the concession process wisely gives the negotiator a tool with as much impact as dollar volume, market conditions, account status, or any other important power-related factor.

Bridging

Bridging is a technique used to eliminate surprise. The introduction of a new demand may create apprehension or even hostility in the supplier. No one likes to be surprised and put off balance by the introduction of a completely unexpected subject. Making a surprise move is potentially dangerous if all has been going along fairly smoothly up until that time.

Therefore, it makes sense for the buyer to do a little preparatory work before raising a new issue. The bridging technique does precisely that — it lays the groundwork for future consideration of an issue. Bridging can be done in many ways, but the simpler the better. One of the most common ways is to refer to the subject in the opening remarks. The buyer should not dwell on it—merely mention it as an area of possible interest and then go on to the next topic. Then, if the subject does appear on the agenda at a later date, it won't be a surprise.

Negotiations tend to fall into a three-step pattern.

The first step is the posturing or bombastic phase, wherein each side attempts to create an atmosphere favorable to its position. In this phase there is no negotiation—no issues are laid on the table, no negotiation limits disclosed. The objective is to avoid any direct reference to the points to be negotiated and establish attitudes, usually tough, to gain some semblance of domination.

The second phase is concerned with determining the potential settlement ranges. Although both sides should have some feel for the potential positions of the other, doubt still remains. It is here that the probing and testing begins to take place. Settlement ranges on the high side are introduced, with expectation that they will be rejected out of hand. The goal is to test the vigor of the response so as to effectively begin to gauge the real settlement areas. Reluctance to introduce high expectation levels at this stage can be fatal. This is the time to begin the psychological battle. Rejection at this stage is expected; the force of the rejection is the information being sought.

The third phase is the concession phase, where the actual agreements begin to develop. It is here that the real work will be done. From the realistic consideration of settlement levels, the final agreement will be hammered out to the satisfaction of both parties. Bridging involves introducing issues in the first two phases to facilitate their resolution in the third phase.

Trial Balloons

Trial ballooning is the tactic of introducing a subject, making a proposal, or stating a demand that has no chance of being accepted. The idea is to test the other side's strength of conviction and general temperament. The buyer may make a demand that is obviously unreasonable, just to see how the other side reacts. For instance, the buyer might introduce a subject that could cause a hostile reaction. If the seller's reaction is mild, the buyer has learned something of the character and attitude of the other side. If the reaction is sharp, the buyer should back off immediately. (The buyer will have found out the seller's feelings, as desired.) This technique should be used sparingly, but be kept in mind for times when it is needed.

Nibbling

Nibbling is the technique of constantly scrambling for small concessions on a given subject. Sometimes, when it becomes clear early in a negotiation that it will be difficult to get the whole package, nibbling makes sense. In the nibbling process, the negotiator patiently breaks the problem into little chunks and goes after the pieces. The basic theory is that it may be possible to negotiate small items one at a time and thus end up with the bulk of the whole. Nibbling is a very common and effective technique.

Good Guy—Bad Guy

The good guy–bad guy technique is one of the oldest gambits in the world. Watch the next detective story on television and the technique will become clear: one detective snarls and attempts to inflict bodily harm on the suspect, only to be restrained by the partner. The partner is the soul of reason and attempts to maintain an atmosphere of calm while questioning the suspect.

In a negotiation, there may be a time to use the good guy–bad guy technique. Before using this technique, the buyer must do some planning. The bad guy must be selected for credibility and acting ability, since this is an acting assignment. The bad guy should be a person of some volatility, who is generally aggressive and dominant. Assigning this job to a mild-mannered person would destroy credibility; everyone would realize that a game was being played.

The purpose of the technique is to unsettle the other side. It is particularly useful in negotiations where there is a definite undertone of latent hostility. If the other side balks on a point and takes a firm stand, it is time to introduce the bad guy. The scenario is simple. Bad guy loses temper, denounces the other side, and storms out of the room. While everyone is still stunned, the good guy attempts to smooth over the situation but, in the process, point out vividly that the whole uproar was caused by the attitude (obviously unreasonable) of the other side on a particular point.

The normal supplier reaction to an outburst will be one of agitation and, in some cases, outright distress. The seller may begin to feel that his or her position was unreasonable. If the bad guy episode manages to do this, it has worked. But, back to the scenario: the good guy calms the group and then persuades a very reluctant bad guy to return to the table. If the bad guy is a good actor, he or she will mumble a halfhearted, completely insincere apology and huffily agree to continue, if people are willing to be reasonable. The objective is to shake up the proceedings in order to get the other side to move from a firm position.

When wisely used, this technique is very effective because it plays on the fact that people wish to avoid confrontation. Discord makes most people uneasy and uncomfortable. When the bad guy reacts violently to the seller's position, it makes the seller reassess this position.

Hostility Relievers

As has been pointed out, the idea in negotiation is to maintain an atmosphere of calm and avoid confrontation if at all possible. However, it is almost inevitable that sometime during a negotiation tension will develop. It is always wise to be prepared with hostility relievers for defusing a situation. Tension relievers range from a change of subject to a break in the proceedings for relaxation. Often a caucus may be called for the purpose of easing things a bit. Taking a break, indulging in light banter, telling appropriate anecdotes, or discussing lighter subjects such as sports is recommended.

Time Usage

Time constraints can and do play an important part in the conduct of a negotiation. Time is an important weapon in the arsenal of the buyer, working with other techniques to achieve concessions. The use of time constraints is a time-honored and effective tactic. There should be a time limit set for any negotiation. Initially it will not appear to influence the procedure. However, as the deadline draws near, the parties begin to realize that if they do not get down to work, there will be a deadlock. The fear of a deadlock is a powerful stimulant to granting concessions and reaching an agreement.

Timing of the buyer's decisive actions is also important. The timing of a caucus can relay an impression of either strength or weakness. The timing of a concession can either emphasize ·time constraints or create the impression that time is no factor to the buyer.

Many people in the United States are not overflowing with patience. This is one reason why they have a hard time learning to negotiate. Impatience is an outgrowth of the type of society we live in. People in the United States tend to be time-oriented. These doers are impatient with delays, eager to get the job done so they can go on to brighter horizons. They have a tremendous awareness of the effect of time on our lives. Opponents in statecraft or business are aware of this national tendency and skillfully use time to gain concessions.

Buyers must learn to play the time game—to consider the use of time in planning and executing the negotiation. Time can be an ally or a worst enemy. If a buyer learns to control time factors, he or she can control the pace of the negotiation and thus, to a certain extent, the concession level.

Silence

Silence is a valid and useful negotiating tactic. To use silence, the buyer must have the discipline to refrain from responding and the ability to totally concentrate on what is being said. An indication of intense interest on the part of the buyer should encourage the speaker to continue. Evidence of disinterest will short-circuit the presentation, to the possible detriment of the buyer.

The Caucus

The caucus has been used in labor negotiations for many years and is just now beginning to attain popularity in industrial negotiations. The timing of a caucus is important; a caucus should not be used when it will leave an impression of weakness or indecision. Deciding when to call a caucus is a matter of discretion for the buyer. Consider some of the following reasons for calling a caucus.

1. Use a caucus when something occurs that changes the balance of power at the negotiating table.

2. Use the caucus to restore discipline in the team. It is not uncommon, in the heat of a negotiation, for members of the team to get embroiled. In so doing, they often forget their roles and discipline dissolves. If this occurs, remedial steps must be taken immediately—the caucus is the format.

3. Use the caucus to develop a plan in the event a major compromise seems to be imminent. Whenever a concession is given, the buyer should be ready with a counterproposal to tie directly to the concession. Since there can be no delays in the making of the counteroffer, preparation and planning are necessary. Regardless of the amount of detailed planning that occurred before the negotiation started, changes will take place and must be recognized and accommodated. The caucus is the vehicle for consideration of the changing situation.

4. Use the caucus to explore alternatives and assess vulnerabilities. No situation is without potential weak points. If the opposition chances on a weak point and exploits it, the

buyer needs a caucus to change plans and shore up defenses. Timing must be considered carefully in this particular situation. If a vulnerable point is touched, the buyer should back off and try to change the subject to a strong point. Once the buyer has regained some semblance of power and control, then he or she can call a caucus. A caucus should never be called in the face of mounting momentum or pressure. This sure indication of a weak position will be quite obvious to the other side.

5. Use the caucus to explore a possible change in tactics or to put together several proposals that are fall-back positions against expected moves by the opposition. This technique of using the caucus to prepare several future positions is very effective. When negotiations have proceeded to a point where it appears that an agreement is imminent, the buyer should have some plan for how to proceed quickly. The idea is to sustain momentum and reach an agreement. The preparation of multiple proposals in anticipation of the seller's proposals permits the buyer to maintain control of the situation. It also puts the burden of decision and response on the shoulders of the seller. The buyer's problem is to control the concessions with counterproposals that provide the best deal for the buyer.

   An added incentive in this technique is that being thoroughly prepared at this late stage of the negotiation will give the buyer a definite psychological advantage. It is unlikely that the sellers will use this tactic, and the display of buyer readiness will pressure the sellers, which should result in favorable concessions to the buyer.

6. Use the caucus to confuse the other side. Here the timing of the caucus is critical. There are no rules on when is the best time to call a caucus, but one must measure the potential impact of a caucus at any given time. One surefire gambit for creating confusion is to call a caucus early in the negotiation when a relatively minor point is on the table. Remember, early in the negotiation both sides are trying to develop facts and seek out the major points in the other side's battle plan. A caucus over a minor point will create considerable confusion in the seller's team and often will result in premature disclosure of information important to the buyer.

7. Use the caucus to gain a chance to rest and to reduce tension. There will be times when it is a good idea to take a break. Ten-

sion may be building that should be defused. Calling a caucus provides the perfect opportunity for both sides to cool off.

Deadlock or "The Hand on the Doorknob"

Deadlock is a condition generally feared by both sides. The deadlock does nothing for either side, yet the threat of a deadlock can be a very powerful negotiating tool. Deadlock is dangerous because it can result in alienation of the parties. The reactions of both sides to a deadlock are much the same; there is definite disappointment at the failure to reach an agreement. Coupled with this are feelings of hostility, which may linger for some time and seriously endanger the future of the buyer-seller relationship.

Before resorting to the threat of deadlock, or indulging in "the hand on the doorknob" approach, consider the rules. Never make people the reason for the walkout. Always make ideas, concepts, a given set of proposals, or lack of proposals the reason. This tactic is loaded with risks. The buyer should be absolutely certain that there is an alternative supplier. If there is no solid alternative and the seller chooses to let the buyer walk, the buyer will be in the unenviable position of having to come back to the table at some future time. If this happens, the seller will be in control of the next negotiation.

Once the buyer has walked out, the buyer must come back to the table only at the initiative of the seller. Once the buyer decides to take the risk of using the threat of a deadlock, there can be no turning back. The gesture of conciliation must come from the seller.

If there is a deadlock, it does not necessarily mean the end of the negotiation, unless so much hostility has developed that the pride of the parties will not permit reconciliation. Therefore, the deadlock and subsequent walkout should be handled as gently as possible, with both parties feeling regret over the development. One should never storm away from the table.

Properly handled, the threat of deadlock can be a powerful tool in the hands of an astute buyer. However, the risk is great, because the threat creates hostility that must be defused immediately, and the buyer must be able to live with the consequences if the gamble fails and an actual walkout takes place.

Remember, nothing in a negotiation is final until both parties decide that it is final. Therefore, there are no rules against either of the parties making overtures to reopen negotiations in a few days. This is more often the case than not. Both sides are usually very uncomfortable after a deadlock, because they would have preferred to reach an agreement. This is why it is so important that the proper atmosphere be maintained in the event of a deadlock. There must be a "bridge" whereby either party can reopen the negotiations with honor intact and without "loss of face."

FINALIZING THE AGREEMENT

The simplest way to document an agreement is to detail the various points as the negotiation proceeds. As each point of agreement is reached, stop in place, develop the language so it is agreeable to both parties, and then have the agreement typed up, signed by both parties, and dated. If this procedure is followed, when the last point has been cleared up the agreement is ready for final typing and signing. This procedure eliminates last-minute changes on points already negotiated.

However, in the event that this procedure cannot be followed, the following suggestions apply:

1. The buyer should take notes continuously during the negotiation, since it is hazardous to rely on memory for recall of points of agreement.
2. There should be a memorandum of agreement prepared prior to the development of the final agreement or formal contract. The meeting should not be adjourned until the memorandum of agreement has been prepared and signed by both parties.
3. Since the memorandum of agreement is an important document that details the understanding of both parties, it is suggested that the buyer take the responsibility for preparing the document. There is method in this madness, because one who prepares the document controls what goes into it. This is not intended to suggest that the preparer of the document attempt to injure or exploit the other party; such a procedure merely ensures that the document is constructed in the way the buyer wants it to be.
4. Face up immediately to problems arising with the memorandum. There will always be some disagreements. Work out such problems at once, regardless of the hour. Do not adjourn because of the lateness of the hour and come back the next day to haggle over the memorandum.

5. If the parties are not sure about a given point, work it out at once. Delay can lead to mind changes, second thoughts, and potential renegotiation of points already settled.

6. Once the bugs have been worked out, have the necessary parties sign the memorandum of agreement.

SUMMARY

The conduct of the negotiation is the final step in the negotiating process and should be one of the most rewarding aspects of the buyer's job.

The two basics that give the buyer power at the negotiating table are dollar volume and knowledge. Of these two, knowledge is the more important. The buyer does not always have dollar volume when negotiating—knowledge will help take up the slack.

The skilled planner of negotiations—and planning is the key to success—will first consider the overall strategy as defined by the objectives sought. Once the strategy has been set, the planner will then determine which tools are needed to achieve these goals. Tactics are selected to reduce the confidence and aspiration level of the opponents while convincing them that their satisfaction levels are being fulfilled.

The preparation of the game plan and the conduct of the negotiation are the culmination of the planning process. The "game plan" includes all of the elements: setting objectives, evaluating the respective power levels of both sides, determining the preferred order of presentation of objectives and using this agenda approach as a control device to keep the negotiations on track, determining what tactical maneuvers will be used during the actual negotiation, deciding what will be covered in the opening statement, determining what concessions will be sought and granted, and deciding how the agreement should be documented.

The documentation process is the final step. If the buyer is satisfied that the maximum has been extracted from a given point, the language agreed to should be written up on the spot, and both parties should sign, date, and time the signing. If, however, there is any doubt as to the final outcome on a point, do not document at that time. Reserve the point and come back to it for further consideration. There is never a need for a hasty concession. Concessions made in haste are generally more generous than those made with deliberation.

As the buyer's experience level grows, this planning will become easier. The conduct of the negotiation will become the major intellectual challenge. There are probably several hundred maneuvers, tactics, and gambits available to the negotiator. The tactics and tools discussed in this chapter are practical and usable by everyone. They take no special training or unusual skills, and they are most certainly sound from a theoretical standpoint.

Patience and silence must be developed. Patience is not a strong point of many people in the United States. The use of silence may force members of the other side to reveal more information than they cared to.

Negotiation is an art and a learned skill. It is the highest form of activity in the buying profession outside of planning. It should be approached with dedication, preparation, high expectation for success, and anticipation of the challenges ahead. A skilled negotiator is a jewel without price.

Glossary of
Basic Purchasing Terms

Acknowledgment: A form used by a vendor to advise the purchaser that the order has been received. It indicates acceptance of the order. Often the required acknowledgment is a second copy of the purchase order.

Act of God: A danger beyond control or avoidance by human power; any accident produced by a physical cause that is irresistible, such as hurricane, flood, or lightning, and is in no way connected with negligence.

Advice of shipment: A notice sent to a purchaser advising that shipment has gone forward. It usually contains details of packing, routing and so on.

Agency: The relation existing between two parties by which one party is authorized to perform or transact certain business for the other; it also applies to the office of the agent. A buyer is normally considered to act as an agent.

Anticipation: An allowance, usually expressed as a percentage, granted for payment of an invoice in advance of the discount or net due date. It is calculated at the stated percentage rate for the number of days between the day of actual payment and the due date, and is allowed in addition to any discounts.

Arbitration: The investigation and resolution of a cause or matter of controversy between parties, by persons chosen with both parties' consent.

Arrival notice: A notice sent by the carrier to the consignee advising of the arrival of a shipment.

As is: A term indicating that goods offered for sale are without warranty or guaranty. The purchaser has no recourse against the vendor for the quality or condition of the goods. Any warranty coverage desired must be negotiated between the parties.

Assignment: Transference of some property right or title to another party. This term is frequently used in connection with bills of lading that are endorsed (assigned) over to another party (the assignee) by the owner of the bill (assignor). Such endorsement gives to the party named the title to the property covered by the bill of lading, and serves to perfect (clear from all encumbrances) title to the goods.

Attachment: A legal proceeding accompanying an action in court by which a plaintiff may require a lien on a defendant's property as security for the payment of any judgment that the plaintiff may obtain.

Authorized deviation: A permission by a buyer to a supplier authorizing the production or delivery, on a restricted basis, of items which deviate from the original specifications or the original terms of the contract or purchase order.

Average demurrage agreement: An agreement made between a shipper and a transportation line whereby the shipper is debited for the time cars are held for loading or unloading beyond a certain period. Demurrage charges are assessed by the transportation line, usually at the end of the month.

Back order: That portion of an order which the vendor cannot deliver at the scheduled time and which is re-entered into the open order file for shipment at a later date.

Barter: The act of exchanging one kind of goods for another, as distinct from trading by the use of money.

Basing point: A particular geographic point to which fixed transportation rates are established. Rates for adjacent points are constructed by adding to, or deducting from, the basing point rate.

Basing rate: A transportation rate on which other rates are constructed or based. For example, the rates from New York to Chicago are the basis from which are constructed rates between points in the east and points in the central territory.

Bid: An offer made in the form of a price, whether for payment or for acceptance. A bid is the quotation given to a prospective purchaser on his or her request, usually in competition with other vendors. It is also an offer by a buyer to a vendor to supply goods at a specified price.

Bill: A form used by a carrier as an invoice, showing consignee, consignor, description of shipment, weight, freight rate, freight charges, and other pertinent information about goods being transported.

Billed weight: The weight shown on the freight bill and waybill, on the basis of which charges are assessed by the carrier.

Bill of lading, uniform: (B/L or b/l): A carrier's contract and receipt for goods that the carrier agrees to transport from one place to another and to deliver to a designated person or assignee for compensation upon such conditions as are stated therein.

The *straight bill of lading* is a nonnegotiable document. It provides for a shipment to be delivered directly to the party whose name is shown as consignee.

The *order bill of lading* is negotiable. Carriers require that this bill be endorsed by the shipper and surrendered upon delivery, in accordance with the terms therein. The object of an order bill of lading is to enable a shipper to collect for the shipment before it reaches its destination. This is done by sending the original bill of lading, with a draft drawn on the consignee, through a bank. The drawee, or the one to whom delivery is made, receives the lading upon payment of the draft and surrenders it to the carrier's agent for the shipment of goods. Customarily, the shipper, when forwarding goods on this form of lading, consigns the shipment to himself or herself, to be delivered only upon his or her order, and designates the person or firm to be notified when the goods arrive at their destination. Upon arrival, shipper, having been paid in advance, assigns shipment to the drawee.

A *clean bill of lading* is one receipted by the carrier for merchandise in good condition (no damage or loss apparent).

An *export bill of lading* is one issued by an inland carrier covering contract of carriage from an interior point of origin to a foreign destination.

A *foul bill of lading* is one indicating that damage or shortage existed at the time of shipment.

A *government bill of lading* is one supplied by the United States government for shipment of government-owned property or for shipment of goods to the government.

An *ocean bill of lading* is one issued by an ocean carrier for marine transport of goods.

Bill of materials: A list specifying the quantity and character of materials and parts required to produce or assemble a stated quantity of a particular product.

Bill of sale: A written agreement under the terms of which the title or interest in a property is transferred by the seller(s) to the buyer or other designated person(s).

Bill of sight: A customhouse document allowing a consignee to see goods before paying duties. Such inspection is made in the presence of a customs officer and is requested by an importer for the purpose of obtaining details in order to prepare a correct bill of entry. The bill of entry must be completed within three days of the bill of sight; otherwise, goods are taken to a government warehouse.

Binder: A tentative but legally enforceable commitment, as by the owner of real property or by a fire insurance company. This may involve payment of earnest money. The binder payment is intended to ensure that the transaction will be completed. Release from a binder or commitment usually results in the buyer's forfeiting the earnest money.

Board: An abbreviation for paperboard. Paperboard is essentially paper, but the term is generally applied to the heavier and thicker grades. The terms board and paperboard cover almost the entire range of forms of paper used in the manufacture of corrugated containers and folding cartons.

Bond performance: A bond executed in connection with a contract, which secures the performance and fulfillment of all the undertakings, covenants, terms, conditions, and agreements contained in the contract. Bonds are frequently used in construction agreements. A bond is really a form of insurance policy which guarantees that one party will perform in a given fashion. Failure to perform results in forfeiture of the bond as recompense for damage to the other party due to the failure to perform.

Bursting strength: The pressure per square inch required to rupture a board sample, as determined by a Mullen or Cady test. Under Federal Rules 41 (freight) and 18 (express), bursting strength must be shown in the boxmaker's certificate.

Buyer's market: Considered to exist when goods can easily be secured and when the economic forces of business cause goods to be priced at the purchaser's estimate of value.

Buyer's option: The privilege of buying a commodity, security, merchandise, or other property within a given period of time, usually at a price and under conditions agreed on in advance of the actual sale. The buyer retains the right not to buy. A seller normally requires a prospective buyer to pay for this option.

Buyer's right of routing: When the seller does not pay freight charges, the buyer has the option of routing. When seller is to prepay freight, the buyer's right of routing must be made a part of the contract of sale; such right should be exercised before actual shipment of goods. If seller disobeys buyer's orders about carriers or routes, he or she incurs all risks of transportation.

Caliper: The thickness of a sheet of board, expressed in thousandths of an inch. In the paper box industry, thousandths of an inch are referred to as points.

C & F (Cost & Freight):   A term used when goods are to be conveyed by ocean marine transportation. It means that the price stated includes both the cost of the goods and the charges for transportation to the named destination point. The seller is liable for the ocean freight charges and for all risks and other charges until he or she has received a clean ocean bill of lading from the carrier (either a "received for shipment" or an "on-board," depending on the agreement between the seller and the buyer), at which point title passes to the buyer. The buyer is liable for all risks and charges, except ocean freight, after title has passed. The buyer is responsible for arranging for insurance on the goods from the point of ocean shipment.

Carload: A quantity of freight to which carload rates apply, or a shipment tendered as a carload.

Carload minimum weight (C/L min):   The least weight at which a shipment is handled at a carload rate.

Carload rate: The rate applying to a carload quantity of freight.

Carton: A term usually used to refer to a folding carton intended as a decorative merchandising package. A carton is not normally used as a shipping container; because it is considered an interior package, it is not designed to meet shipping standards.

Cash in advance: Same as cash with order.

Cash on delivery (C.O.D.):   Payment due and payable upon delivery of goods.

Cash with order: Payment accompanies order.

Caveat emptor: "Let the buyer beware"—the purchase is at the buyer's risk.

Caveat venditor: "Let the seller beware"—the seller is liable to the buyer if the goods delivered are different in kind, quality, use, and purpose from those described in the contract of sale.

Certificate of compliance: A supplier's certification to the effect that the supplies or services in question meet specified requirements.

Certificate of damage: A document issued by dock companies stating that merchandise has been received or unloaded in a damaged condition. It serves as a notice to the consignee regarding the condition of the goods.

Certificate of origin: A certified document specifying the origin of goods.

Certificate of weight: An authoritative statement of the weight of a shipment, usually certified by the agency that weighed the goods.

Certified bill of lading: An ocean bill of lading certified by a consular officer to meet requirements of the consul's country for goods imported.

Certified check: A check drawn on a bank and accepted by it. A certified check is drawn only after funds to cover have been deposited in the bank issuing the check.

Change order: A purchaser's document used to amend a purchase transaction previously formalized by a purchase order.

Chattel: A very broad term encompassing every kind of property that is not land. The word "chattel" is derived from the word "cattle."

Check: A bill of exchange or draft drawn on a bank and payable on demand.

C.I.F. (Cost, Insurance & Freight):   Similar to C & F (cost and freight), except the cost of ocean marine insurance is also paid by the seller. "War risk" insurance is usually charged to the buyer.

Classification of purchaser: Vendor's assignment of a purchaser to a category for the purpose of determining prices or discounts. Typical classifications are ultimate consumer, retailer, wholesaler, distributor, and original equipment manufacturer.

Collateral: Security placed with a creditor to ensure performance of an obligation. Any property with a value equal to the amount of the obligation is acceptable collateral. The basic assumption is that if the obligation is not met, the collateral can be sold to satisfy the obligation.

Commercial law: That branch of the law used to designate the rules that determine the rights and duties of persons engaged in trade and commerce.

Commodity rate: A general rate applicable to transport to, from, or between specific points of articles described or named in the tariff.

Common carrier: A person or corporation licensed by an authorized state, federal, or other governmental agency to transport personal property from one place to another for compensation. A common carrier is bound to carry for all who tender their goods and the price of transportation.

Common law: Unwritten law based on precedent expressed in judicial decisions, from early decisions in England to recent decisions in the United States.

Competitive bidding: The offering of estimates by individuals or firms competing for a contract, privilege, or right to supply specified services or merchandise.

Compromise: An agreement among two or more persons to settle a controversy without resort to litigation.

Condemnation proceedings: An action or proceeding in court for the purpose of taking private property for public use.

Conditional sale: A sale in which title is retained by the vendor as security until the complete purchase price has been paid, although possession of the article is surrendered to the buyer.

Confirming order: A purchase order issued to a vendor, confirming and listing the goods or services and terms of an order placed verbally or otherwise.

Consideration: Something of value given to make a promise binding. Consideration is sometimes called a binder or earnest money.

Consignee: The person or organization to whom the carrier delivers goods, as directed by the shipper. This person or organization is generally the buyer of goods.

Consignment: Goods shipped for future sale or other purpose. The title remains with the shipper (consignor), although the receiver (consignee), upon acceptance of the goods, is accountable for them. Consigned goods are a part of the consignor's inventory until sold. The consignee may be the eventual purchaser, may act as the agent through whom the sale is effected, or may otherwise dispose of the goods in accordance with the agreement with the consignor.

Consignor: The person or organization who delivers freight to a carrier for shipment; the shipper. This person draws up the bill of lading to be executed by the carrier. A person or organization may be a consignor-consignee if the bill of lading is made to the order of the consignor.

Constructive delivery: Delivery of personal property through passage of possession and title where physical delivery has not occurred. Passage is inferred from the conduct of the parties.

Container: An item in which or around which another item or items are kept. It is maintained as an entity mainly for shipping or issue purposes. Examples: corrugated carton, barrel, bottle, can, drum, reel, spool.

Continuing guaranty: A commitment by one person to another person that the first person may be held liable for payment of money to be loaned or goods to be sold to a third person. The principal accepts future liability for a series of future transactions. It is usually revocable with respect to all future transactions upon actual notice.

Contract: A deliberate agreement among two or more competent persons to perform or not to perform a specific act or acts. A contract may be verbal or written. A purchase order, when accepted by a vendor, becomes a contract. Acceptance may be either in writing or by performance, unless the purchase order requires acceptance to be in writing. A *unilateral contract* is one where only one party promises performance, the performance being in exchange for an act by the other. A *bilateral contract* is one where both parties promise, each promise being given in exchange for the other.

Contract carrier: Any person or corporation not designated as a common carrier who, under special and individual contracts or agreements, transports passengers or property by motor vehicle for compensation.

Contract date: The date on which a contract is accepted by all parties thereto.

Contractor: (1) Any one of the parties to a contract. (2) One who contracts to perform work or furnish materials in accordance with a contract.

Conveyance: (1) A formal written instrument, usually called a deed, by which the title or other interest in land (real property) is transferred from one person to another. (2) The equipment in which goods are transported by a carrier, such as railroad car, truck, vessel, barge, airplane, and so on.

Conveyor: A generic term for a class of materials-handling devices used to move things over a fixed line of travel. Examples: conveyor lines in a plant to move goods, drag lines in mining operations.

Corporation: A collection of individuals authorized by statute to act as a legal person, vested with the power and capacity to contract, own, control, convey property, and transact business within the limits of the powers granted.

Cost-plus method: A pricing method whereby the purchaser agrees to pay the vendor the costs incurred by the vendor in producing the goods and/or services plus a stated percentage or fixed sum as profit.

Counteroffer: An offer to enter into a transaction on terms differing from those first proposed. Any acceptance of an offer with terms that materially change the nature of the offer constitutes a counteroffer. If the offeror accepts the revised terms, these terms will control the agreement.

Covenant: A promise in writing under seal. This term is often used as a substitute for the word "contract."

Currency: Lawful money in current circulation. The terms "currency" and "current funds" include not only coin, silver, United States notes, and treasury notes, but also silver certificates, Federal Reserve notes, and national bank notes.

Cwt: See *Hundredweight.*

Cylinder: One of two principal types of board machines or board produced on a cylinder machine. The other principal type is a fourdrinier. The cylinder machine uses a batch system, usually converting recycled materials into paper.

Damages: Compensation, usually in money, for injury to goods, person, or property.

Dating (delayed billing):   A method of granting extended credit terms. This method is used by sellers to induce buyers to accept goods in advance of the required delivery date, thus permitting the seller to ship goods earlier than the buyer would ordinarily wish to receive them.

Debt: Any obligation to pay money. Ordinarily the term debt means a sum of money due by reason of a contract expressed or implied. Broadly, the word may include obligations other than money due, such as the duty to render services or deliver goods.

Declared valuation: The monetary value placed on a shipment when it is delivered to the carrier.

Deed: A written instrument in a special form that is used to pass the legal title of real property from one person to another. See *Conveyance.* In order that the public may know about the title to real property, deeds are recorded in the deed record office of the county or town where the land is situated.

Delivery: The transfer of possession. As applied to shipping, delivery occurs when the bill of lading is surrendered and the title to goods is passed to the receiver or consignee.

Delivery schedule: The required or agreed time or rate of delivery of goods or services purchased for a future period.

Demurrage: A charge, allowed in tariffs or by contract, assessed against a consignor, consignee, or other responsible person for delays to transportation equipment in excess of free time for loading, unloading, reconsigning, or stopping in transit.

Demurrage agreement: An agreement between a carrier and a consignor (or consignee) whereby delays in excess of the allowed free time provided in the tariffs are debited against the consignor (or consignee), and delays less than those allowed are credited to the consignor (or consignee). In rail-carrier demurrage agreements, charges are assessed by the carrier on the net debits on a periodic basis, usually at the end of a month.

Deposition: The written testimony of a witness taken in proper form, under oath. Usually a deposition is part of the pretrial discovery process and involves the presence of counsel for both sides and a court reporter.

Depreciation: Decline in value of a capital asset through wear and tear, age, inadequacy, and obsolescence, without loss of substance.

Destination: The place to which a shipment is consigned.

Discount: An allowance or deduction granted by the seller to the buyer which reduces the cost of the goods purchased. Discounts usually are granted when certain stipulated conditions are met by the buyer. However, discounts may be granted without reference to stipulated conditions. An example of such use of discount is the application of discount to a nominal or "list" price to establish the "net" or actual price.

An *arbitrary discount* is one agreed upon by vendor and purchaser which has no relation to the vendor's usual basis for discount.

A *broken package discount* is one that applies to a quantity of goods less than the quantity contained in a vendor's regular package.

A *cash discount* is an allowance extended to encourage payment of invoice before a stated date which is earlier than the net date. The percent of discount allowed is agreed on by the buyer and the seller and may be established by industry or trade custom.

- 1 percent ten days net 30—means that if the buyer pays the invoice within 10 days, a 1 percent discount on the invoice is allowed. The entire invoice is due in 30 days.
- 1 percent e.o.m.—means that a 1 percent discount will be allowed if the buyer pays on or before the end of the month.
- 2 percent e.o.m.–10—means that a 2 percent discount will be allowed if buyer pays on or before the tenth of the following month.
- 2 percent 10–60X or 2 percent 10–60 extra—means that a 2 percent discount will be allowed if buyer pays on or before the seventieth day.
- 2 percent 10th prox—means the same as 2 percent e.o.m.–10.
- 2 percent 10th & 25th or 2 percent 25th & 10th—means that a 2 percent discount will be allowed for payment on or before the twenty-fifth of the month for billings of the first half of the month, and a 2 percent discount will be allowed for payment on or before the tenth of the succeeding month for billings of the last half of the month.

Discount payment dates other than those with e.o.m. or prox terms are interpreted in various ways. The usual interpretation is that the discount date is calculated from the invoice date. The buyer and the seller should specifically agree on any other interpretation. Other interpretations may be based on (a) the date goods are shipped, (b) the date goods are received by the buyer, and (c) the date goods are inspected and found acceptable by the buyer. Discount payment terms usually are stated in conjunction with a net term. Typical terms are:

- 1 percent 10 days, net 30 (or 1–10–30)
- 2 percent 10 days, net 60 (or 2–10–60)
- 2 percent 10 days, 60 extra, net 90 (or 2–10–60X, net 90)
- 2 percent 30, net 31

Where the net date is not stated in conjunction with a discount date, the presumption is that the invoice is due net the day following the discount date. Net terms require that vendor's invoices be paid without discount on or before due date. Typical statements of net terms are

- Net—payment due immediately.
- Net 10 days—payment due on or before the tenth day.
- Net e.o.m.—payment due on or before the end of the month.
- Net e.o.m. 10, net 10 e.o.m., or net 10th prox—payment due on or before the tenth of the month following.
- Net 10–60X or net 10–60 extra—payment due on or before the seventieth day.
- Net 10th & 25th or net 25th & 10th—payment due on the twenty-fifth of the month for billings of the first half of the month; payment due on the tenth of the following month for billings of the last half of the month.

A *chain discount* is a series of discounts. The percent of each discount in the chain applies to the amount resulting from application of the immediately preceding percent of discount. For example, consider a 20 percent–10 percent chain discount on an amount of $100. The 20 percent discount on $100 would leave $80; then a 10 percent discount on the $80 would leave $72.

A *quantity discount* is an allowance determined by the quantity or value of a purchase.

A *standard package discount* is one that applies to goods supplied in the vendor's regular package.

A *trade discount* is a deduction from an established price made by the seller to those engaged in certain businesses and allowed irrespective of when payment is made. It often varies in percentage according to the volume of the transaction.

Discount schedule: The list of discounts applying to differing quantities of goods or to differing classifications of purchasers.

Draft: A written order drawn by one party (drawer) ordering a second party (drawee) to pay a specified sum of money to a third party (payee). A *sight draft* is payable upon presentation to the drawee. An *arrival draft* is prepared by the seller and, with invoice and shipping receipt for the goods sold, is deposited at the seller's bank for collection. The bank forwards the documents to its correspondent bank in the buyer's city. The buyer secures the invoice and shipping receipt from the bank upon payment or acceptance of the draft, usually when the goods arrive at the destination. A *time draft* is payable at a stated time *after* acceptance by the drawee.

Drawback: A refund of customs duties paid on material imported and later exported. Drawbacks are standard procedure in the sugar business.

Due care: The standard of conduct that is exercised by an ordinary, reasonable, prudent person.

Duty: A tax levied by a government on the importation, exportation, or use and consumption of goods.

Earnest money: Money that one contracting party gives to another at the time they enter into the contract, in order to "bind the bargain." The money is forfeited by the donor if he or she fails to carry out the contract. Generally, in real estate contracts, such money is used as part payment of the purchase price. It is also called a binder.

Embargo: An order issued by a carrier, carrier's agent, or government, prohibiting the acceptance of freight, in any kind or of a specific nature, for shipment. Generally an embargo applies to shipments to and from particular points, and is the result of congestion, labor troubles, and so on. In marine usage, it is a detention of vessels in port, a prohibition from sailing.

En route: On the way; in transit.

Escalator: An amount or percent by which a contract price may be adjusted if specified contingencies occur, such as changes in the vendor's raw material or labor costs.

Escrow: An agreement under which a grantor, promisor, or obligor places a sum of money or the instrument (such as a bond or a deed) upon which he or she is bound with a third person, called the escrow holder, until the performance of a condition or the happening of an event, as stated in the agreement, permits the escrow holder to deliver the money or instrument to the grantee, promisee, or obligee.

Expedite: To hasten or to ensure delivery of goods purchased in accordance with a time schedule, usually a part of the contract between the purchaser and the vendor.

Express warranty: Warranty made when a seller makes some positive representation concerning the nature, quality, character, use, and purpose of goods, which induces the buyer to buy and which the seller intends the buyer to rely on. The key is the fact that the representations made as to quality or performance were the influencing factors causing the buyer to purchase the item.

Factor: An agent for the sale of merchandise who holds possession of the goods in his or her own name or in the name of the principal. The factor is authorized to sell and to receive payment for the goods.

Fair market value: The value of an item, as determined through negotiation between the buyer and the seller. This value would normally determine the purchase price.

FAS (Free alongside ship):   Abbreviation indicating that the seller is liable for all charges and risks until the goods sold are delivered alongside a vessel at the named port or are delivered to a dock which will be used by the vessel. The term FAS must be qualified by a named port. Title passes to the buyer when the seller has secured a ship's receipt for the goods.

Fifo: First in, first out; refers to accounting, handling, and pricing of materials held in inventories.

Finder: A person who acts to bring together a purchaser and a vendor and who is not in the employ of either. A finder usually is paid a fee by the party engaging this service.

Firm offer: A definite proposal to sell something on stated terms, binding the proposer until a stipulated time of expiration. A *firm bid* is a similar proposal to buy something.

Floor-load capacity: The maximum weight that the floor in a particular location in a building can safely support, expressed in pounds per square foot.

FOB (Free on board):   An abbreviation indicating that the seller is required to place the goods aboard the equipment of the transporting carrier without charge to the buyer. The term FOB must be qualified by the name of a location, such as a shipping point or a destination. The location may be the name of a city, mill, or warehouse. The stated FOB point is usually the location where title to the goods passes from the seller to the buyer. The seller is liable for transportation charges and the risks of loss or damage to the goods up to the point where title passes to the buyer. The buyer is liable for such charges and risks after the passage of the title.

FOR (Free on rails):   An abbreviation indicating that the seller must deliver to the railroad terminal named or, in the case of overseas shipment, to the harbor at the named port of departure. Since this term is often considered to be the equivalent of "FOB vessel ____," or "FAS vessel ____," the phrase may be amplified further to avoid misunderstanding; thus, "FOR, cartage to vessel extra."

Fourdrinier: One of the two principal types of paper or board machines, the other type being the cylinder. The fourdrinier paper machine is a continuous flow machine that starts with wood chips and converts them into paper.

Free goods: Goods not subject to duty.

Free port: A restricted area at a seaport for the handling of duty-exempted import goods; a "foreign trade zone."

Freight at destination: Freight charges are paid by the consignee of goods upon their arrival at a specified destination.

Futures: Contracts for the sale and delivery of commodities at a future time, made with the intention that no commodity be delivered or received immediately.

Good title: A title free from encumbrances such as mortgages and liens.

Grain: The direction in which individual fibers tend to be aligned. Paper or paperboard made on modern high-speed machines has grain roughly comparable to the grain of wood. In the formation of the sheet on the machine, the individual fibers tend to be aligned in machine direction more than in cross-machine direction, thus producing grain in machine direction.

Gross negligence: The absence of even slight care.

Hedge: Any purchase or sales transaction made with the purpose of eliminating profit or loss arising from price fluctuations. Specifically, a hedge is a purchase or sale used to balance the costs of a sale or purchase already made, or to offset the effect of price fluctuation in a contract.

Hundredweight (cwt):   In U.S. measurement and in domestic rail freight, a hundredweight equals 100 pounds; in English measurement and in ocean freight parlance, a hundredweight is 112 pounds, or one-twentieth of a long ton of 2240 pounds. The negotiator should take care when using this phrase that there is no confusion about the exact meaning.

Import: To receive goods from a foreign country.

Importer: A buyer or merchant who imports goods.

In bond: In the custody of a warehouse or carrier, from whom the goods can be taken only after payment of taxes or duties to a government agency.

Inventory: (1) The amount of property on hand at any given time. (2) An itemized listing of amounts of property indicated as being on hand at a particular time. A *physical inventory* is one determined by actual physical count of the items. A *book inventory* is one determined from records maintained in connection with day-to-day business activities.

Invitation for bids: A request, verbal or written, made to suppliers for their quotations on goods or services desired by the prospective purchaser.

Invoice: A document showing the character, quantity, price, terms, nature of delivery, and other particulars of goods sold or of services rendered; a bill.

Jobber: A middleman or dealer who purchases goods or commodities from manufacturers or importers and sells them to retailers. A jobber is also called a dealer or a wholesale merchant.

KD (knocked down):   An abbreviation meaning that the article described is supplied unassembled. When an article is shipped at KD rate, it must be reduced in size by one-third or as specified in the carrier's tariff.

Kraft: A paper or board made from virgin pulp, in a paper-pulping process involving sulfate.

Landed price: A price that includes the cost of the goods, transportation, and other incidentals involved in the ultimate delivery of the goods to the location specified by the purchaser.

Lead time: The period of time, from date of ordering to date of delivery, that the buyer must allow for the vendor to prepare goods for shipment.

Lease: A contract conveying real estate or personal property from one person (lessee) to another (lessor) for a term, in return for a specified rent or other compensation.

Legal tender: Currency or coin that a government has declared shall be received in payment of duties or debts.

Less-than-carload (lcl):   A quantity of freight that is less than the amount necessary to constitute a carload.

Less-than-carload rate: A rate applicable to a shipment of less than a carload.

Less-than-truckload (ltl)   A quantity of freight that is less than the amount necessary to constitute a truckload.

Less-than-truckload rate: A rate applicable to a shipment of less than a truckload.

Letter of intent: A preliminary contractual arrangement customarily used in situations where the items, quantities, price, and delivery dates are known, but where the principal contract provisions require additional time-consuming negotiations. It is used as an interim agreement, pending a definitive contract, in order to permit the start of construction, production, or delivery of the supplies or materials.

Lien: The right of one person, usually a creditor, to keep possession or control of the property of another, for the purpose of satisfying a debt.

Lifo: Last in, first out; refers to accounting, handling, and pricing of materials held in inventories.

Marketable title: A title of such character that no apprehension about its validity would occur in the mind of a reasonable and intelligent person.

Mechanic's lien: A lien created by statute to insure laborers for their wages. The purpose of this lien is to subject the land of an owner to a lien for the cost of materials and labor expended in the construction of buildings. Once buildings have been placed on the land, they become part of the lien by the law of accession.

Mortgage: A lien on land, buildings, machinery, equipment, or other fixed or movable property, given to the seller by a buyer as security for payment of the purchase price, or given to a lender by a borrower as security for a loan. A *real estate mortgage* applies to land and buildings. A *chattel mortgage* applies to all other types of property.

Mullen test: A test of the pressure required to puncture a paper sample under specific conditions, performed on a piece of testing equipment known as a Mullen tester. The Mullen test is required in connection with various shipping regulations.

Mutual assent: Agreement of each party to the same thing. In every contract, each must know what the other intends.

Negligence: The failure to do that which an ordinary, reasonable, prudent person would do, or the performance of some act that an ordinary, prudent person would not do. Reference must always be made to the situation, the circumstances, and the knowledge of the parties.

Open-account purchase: A purchase made by a buyer who has established credit with the seller. Payment terms usually require payment of invoice in full on or before a specific date or dates, or deduction of a certain percentage for prompt payment. Such terms are agreed to by the buyer and seller either before or at the time an order is placed.

Open-to-buy: The maximum value or quantity of goods a buyer is authorized to purchase; the value or quantity remaining to be purchased against a specific appropriation requisition or budget or production requirement.

Packaging: The use of wrappings, cushioning materials, containers, markings, and the like to protect items from deterioration, to prevent loss or damage, to facilitate handling, and to identify the item packaged. Packaging does not include additional processing which may be required to prepare the packaged item for shipment.

Packing: The preparation of an item for shipment or storage; this includes required bracing, cushioning, wrapping, strapping, placing in shipping containers, and marking.

Packing list: A document that itemizes in detail the contents of a particular package or shipment.

Point of origin: The point or place at which the transportation line receives a shipment from the shipper.

Prepaid: A term indicating that transportation charges have been or are to be paid at the point of shipment.

Price prevailing at date of shipment: An agreement between the purchaser and the vendor that the price of the goods ordered is subject to change at the vendor's discretion between the date the order is placed and the date the vendor makes shipment, and that the then-established price is the contract price.

Price protection: An agreement between a vendor and a purchaser which grants the purchaser any reduction in price that the vendor may establish on goods prior to shipment of the purchaser's order. Price protection is sometimes extended beyond the date of shipment.

Price schedule: The list of prices applying to varying quantities or kinds of goods.

Pro forma invoice: An invoice prepared by a vendor in advance of a sale to show the form and amount of the invoice that will be rendered to the purchaser, if the sale is consummated. Pro forma invoices are often used in export transactions to support the purchaser's request to governmental authorities for import permits and foreign exchange.

Progress payments: Periodic payments in advance of delivery, arranged in connection with transactions. Payments are in named amounts or certain percentages of the purchase price. The whole of the purchase price may be due in advance of delivery, or part may be due in advance and part after delivery. Progress payments are usually required in contracts for building construction and often for specially designed plant machinery and equipment. Purchases calling for progress payments may be either on an open account or secured, usually by a contract between the buyer and seller.

Promissory note: An unconditional written promise, signed by the maker, to pay a certain sum in money, on demand or at a fixed or determinable future date, either to the bearer or to a designated person.

Pro-number: Agent's number, with the prefix pro- (derived from the word "progressive"), placed on freight bills so that a specific consignment may be referred to instantly.

Purchase: To procure property or services for a price. This includes obtaining by barter.

Purchase order: The purchaser's document used to formalize a purchase transaction with a vendor. It should contain statements about the quantity, description, and price of the goods or services ordered; payment terms and discounts; date of performance; transportation terms; and all other agreements pertinent to the purchase and its execution by the vendor.

Purchase requisition: An internal form used to request that the purchasing department procure goods or services from vendors. It can be called a traveling purchase requisition.

Quotation: A statement of price, terms of sale, and description of goods or services offered by a vendor to a prospective purchaser; a bid. When a bid is given in response to an inquiry, it is usually considered an offer to sell. Also, it is the stating of the current price of a commodity or the price so stated.

Rebate: A sum of money returned by the vendor to a purchaser in consideration of the purchase of a stipulated quantity or value of goods, usually within a stated period.

Receiving report: A form used by the receiving department of a company to inform others of the receipt of goods purchased. Usually copies are distributed to the purchasing and accounting departments and the storerooms.

Retention: The practice of withholding a portion of the sum due a vendor until the purchase has been finally accepted as fully meeting specifications. At the time of purchase, the parties should agree on the amount or percentage to be withheld and the period of retention.

Royalty: Compensation paid to the owner, vendor, or lessor for the use of land, equipment, or process. Royalty payments are usually calculated as a percentage of the income derived by the user from the property or process, as a stated sum per unit produced therefrom, or as a stated sum per period, such as per month or year.

Sales tax: A tax imposed specifically on a sale made by a vendor.

Salvage: (1) Property that has some value in addition to its value as scrap, but which is no longer useful in its present condition as a unit and which could not economically be restored to usefulness as a unit. (2) The act of saving or recovering condemned, discarded, or abandoned property in order to obtain useful parts and scrap therefrom.

Sample: A small portion of merchandise taken as a specimen of quality.

Scrap: Material that has no value except for its basic material content.

Seller's lien: The right of a seller to retain possession of goods until the buyer pays. This right does not exist where goods are sold on credit.

Seller's market: Considered to exist when goods cannot easily be secured and when the economic forces of business cause goods to be priced at the vendor's estimate of value.

Short sale: The sale of a commodity that the seller does not possess but intends to purchase prior to the required delivery date, expecting that the market price will be no higher or will decline during the period before the delivery date.

Specifications: A clear, complete, and accurate statement of the technical requirements to be met by a material, an item, or a service, and of the procedure to be followed in determining if these requirements are met. *Federal specifications* are those established by governmental agencies in accordance with procedures prescribed by the Federal Specifications Board.

Stock: A supply of goods maintained on hand at the storage points in a supply system to meet anticipated demands.

S.U. (Setup):   An abbreviation meaning that the article so described is supplied fully assembled.

Subcontractor: A party who contracts with a prime contractor to perform all or any part of the prime contractor's obligations in a particular prime contract.

Terms of payment: Manner in which the seller is compensated by the buyer for the goods or services the latter receives through a purchase transaction. Except in the cases of an unusual exchange or barter deal, payment is made in negotiable funds in accordance with the terms agreed to by buyer and seller. There are three basic payment terms: cash, open account, and secured account.

Trademark: Generally, any sign, mark, symbol, word, or arrangement of words in the form of a label, which is adopted and used by a manufacturer or distributor to designate the company's particular goods and which no other person has the legal right to use. Originally, the design or trademark indicated origin, but today it is used more often as an advertising mechanism.

Trade terms: Understandings between buyer and seller, either as to the meanings of certain abbreviations, words, or phrases or as to the customs applicable to the transactions, as established by agreement between the parties or by general usage. Trade terms include agreed upon or arbitrary classifications of buyers and sellers or their agents; types and methods of discounts, delivery terms, allowances; and practices peculiar to an industry.

Traveling purchase requisition: A purchase requisition designed for repetitive use. After a purchase order has been prepared for the goods requisitioned, the form is returned to the originator, who holds it until a repurchase of the goods is required. The name is derived from the repetitive travel of the form between the originating and purchasing departments.

Vendee: A purchaser of property. The term is generally applied to the purchaser of real property, while the word buyer is usually applied to the purchaser of personal property.

Vendor: One who sells something; a seller.

Vendor's lien: An unpaid seller's right to hold possession of property until he or she has recovered the purchase price.

Visual inspection: Inspection performed without the aid of test instruments.

Voucher: A written instrument that bears witness or "vouches" for something. Generally, a voucher authorizes payment to the vendor and shows that services were performed or that goods were purchased.

Warranty: An undertaking, either expressed or implied, that a certain fact regarding the subject matter of a contract is presently true or will be true. Warranty should be distinguished from guaranty, which means a contract or promise by one person to answer for the performance of another.

Waybill: A document prepared by a transportation line at the point of origin of a shipment, showing the point of origin, destination, route, consignor, consignee, description of shipment, and amount charged for the transportation service. This document is forwarded to the carrier's agent at the transfer point or destination. An *astray waybill* is used for freight miscarried or separated from its proper waybill. A *blanket waybill* is one covering two or more consignments of freight. An *interline waybill* is one covering the movement of freight over two or more transportation lines.

Weight, gross: The weight of an article together with the weight of its container and the material used for packing.

Weight, net: The actual weight of the contents of a container or of the cargo of a vehicle. It is the total weight less the tare weight.

Weight, tare: The weight of an empty container and any other material used for packing its contents. *Actual tare* is determined when each cask, bag, or the like is weighed; *average tare,* when one is weighed as a sample; and *estimated tare,* when a fixed percentage is allowed.

Wholesaler: A purchaser who acquires goods for resale to a retailer or a jobber.

Index